WITHDRAWN

hardware Style

hardware Style

100 Creative Decorating Ideas Using Materials from Every Aisle of the Home Center Store

LARK BOOKS

A Division of Sterling Publishing Co., Inc.

New York

Marthe Le Van

Art Director: Tom Metcalf
Cover Designer: Barbara Zaretsky
Art Assistant: Shannon Yokeley
Production Assistant: Lorelei Buckley, Avery Johnson
Editorial Assistance: Heather Smith, Delores Gosnell
Photographer: keithwright.com
Illustrator: Orrin Lundgren
Proofreader: Sherry Hames

Special Photography
Sanoma Syndication: Rene Gonkel, pages 39, 64, 65, 96, and 97; John van Groenedaal, page 59; Peter Kooijman pages 34, 35, and 88; Brigitte Kroone, page 38; Paul Steenbakker, page 138; Louis Lemaire, page 87; Eric van Lokven, pages 54 and 55; Dennis Brandsma, pages 86 and 107; Paul Grootes, pages 82 and 83; and Ewout Huibers, page 19.

Library of Congress Cataloging-in-Publication Data

Le Van, Marthe.
  Hardware style : 100 creative decorating ideas using materials from
every aisle of the home center store / by Marthe Le Van.
      p. cm.
  ISBN 1-57990-420-3 (hardcover)
 1. Handicraft. 2. Interior decoration. 3. House furnishings. I.
Title.
  TT157.L429 2003
  745.5--dc21

                    2002154663

10 9 8 7 6 5 4 3 2 1

First Edition

Published by Lark Books, a division of
Sterling Publishing Co., Inc.
387 Park Avenue South, New York, N.Y. 10016

© 2003, Lark Books

Distributed in Canada by Sterling Publishing,
c/o Canadian Manda Group, One Atlantic Ave., Suite 105
Toronto, Ontario, Canada M6K 3E7

Distributed in the U.K. by Guild of Master Craftsman Publications Ltd.
Castle Place, 166 High Street Lewes, East Sussex, England BN7 1XU
Tel: (+ 44) 1273 477374, Fax: (+ 44) 1273 478606
 Email: pubs@thegmcgroup.com Web: www.gmcpublications.com

Distributed in Australia by Capricorn Link (Australia) Pty Ltd.,
P.O. Box 704, Windsor, NSW 2756 Australia

If you have questions or comments about this book, please contact:
Lark Books
67 Broadway
Asheville, NC 28801
(828) 253-0467

Manufactured in China

ISBN 1-57990-420-3

contents

introduction

Hardware style is an exciting decorating trend that uses materials from all parts of the home center store in imaginative and unconventional ways. Because home improvement centers are so vast, and their inventories so diverse, you can find inspiring bits and pieces on every aisle, and then use them as fashionable interior accents. All you have to do is visualize the merchandise not for what it actually is, but for what it could be; every single item is open to creative reinterpretation.

One of today's most acclaimed decorating practices is *repurposing*. This fashionable buzzword means taking items conceived for one purpose and using them in an entirely different way. Nowhere is this movement more successfully played out than in the pursuit of hardware style, and "played out" could not be a more appropriate phrase. It's delightful to recognize the innate beauty and design potential in an otherwise common

object. This book encourages you to appreciate a handsome bolt or a lustrous chain, not only for its practical abilities, but also for its aesthetic appeal. Even if you use words like *thingamajig* and *whatchamacallit* to describe them, home center supplies can quickly become your most valuable decorating assets.

Our strategy for introducing hardware style was two-fold: first, loosely base the book's layout on a home improvement center floor plan, and then challenge designers to make home accents from *every* department. From plumbing to hardware, electrical to lawn and garden, our creative team was summoned to leave no section unexplored, and the results are amazing. They

brought forth more than 100 ideas and projects in a wide range of design styles for every type of decorator in every type of home. Now it's your turn to reap the benefits of their ambitious pursuit. Whether you enter the store with one of our supply lists firmly in hand or simply in search of artistic inspiration, take time to look closely at the contour, color, finish, and proportions of the

items you'll see all around you. You're sure to spot irresistible elements to add to your decor.

At the beginning of every chapter we give you a brief overview of the featured home center department in the form of a buying guide, introducing you to that department's unique materials. We tell you what they're traditionally used for and hint at how they make the transition into hardware-style home decor. Throughout the book are carefully selected tips and hints for working with the most popular home center supplies. There are also techniques for successfully assembling and safely installing your designs.

Thanks to accessible materials and easy-to-understand instructions, you can quickly enhance your environment. Most of the decorating ideas in this book require very little labor. For example, your most daunting task may be shopping for the most appealing planter, hardware organizer, drawer pull, or utility hook; bringing it home; and putting it to use. Many projects are simply slight

modifications to an off-the-shelf item, such as applying a fresh coat of paint or attaching a set of wired-on washers. In a few instances, you'll need to know some basic do-it-yourself techniques, such as sewing, sawing, or finding a stud.

Whether your style is boldly modern or classically refined, you'll love making home center accessories. Influenced by urban renewal, yet appropriate for any setting, these projects and ideas convey authentic design ingenuity with a distinctly modern charm. Why settle for mass-produced merchandise that doesn't reflect your own individual style? Let the home center be your principal source for artful living.

Tool & Hardware Departments

Tool and hardware departments stock the most essential home improvement merchandise. No matter how large modern warehouse centers grow, you'll still find tools and hardware at their core. On these particular aisles, you'll encounter row upon row of do-it-yourself gadgets, from large power tools to tiny fasteners. These are required items for professional builders or budding DIY enthusiasts to get their jobs done—literally the "tools of the trade." When you peruse the aisles with a different eye, one focused on creative decor opportunities, the tool and hardware departments become a vast treasure trove of inspiration.

Fasteners

This is the hardware for holding everything together. While combing these aisles you'll uncover nuts, bolts, screws, nails, and hooks in every size and shape imaginable. Esoteric coatings, ends, materials, and heads make fasteners even more engaging. To witness firsthand the awesome variety, just spend some time opening up the many bins, boxes, and drawers on this aisle. You won't be disappointed.

Cabinet Hardware

Recently, there has been a cabinet-hardware renaissance. Manufacturers are producing more attractive knobs, pulls, and hinges than ever before, and the public just can't seem to get enough of the new and improved designs. Metal cabinet hardware is offered in copper, chrome, brass, nickel, bronze, and iron. You can opt for a brushed, polished, or high-gloss finish. Glass, ceramic, plastic, and wood varieties help fill out the options on this ever-expanding aisle. Most cabinet hardware is sold with a proper fastener, making it an extremely easy element to incorporate into decor projects.

Rope, Chain & Cable

Typically, these three kinds of flexible line fasteners are used to bear weight and secure objects in place. In addition to this noble duty, rope, chain, and cable also can be put to decorative use. From the rugged handsomeness of a thick hemp rope to the post-industrial flair of a bright zinc chain, there's a line suitable for any interior project.

Hardware Holders

From multi-drawer plastic cabinets to industrial strength hand-held chests, there are hardware holders built for every conceivable purpose. Whether they're intended for organizing tiny fasteners in a home workshop, or routinely transporting power tools between job sites, these diverse hardware holders also carry a lot of promise as stylish home accessories.

Springs

All springs are just coiled wire, but not all springs are created equally. The thickness of the wire, the tightness and length of the coil, and the shape of the wire end determines a spring's use. Tightly coiled springs with hooks on the ends are designed to expand; loosely coiled springs with plain or cut-off ends are made to compress. However you choose to use a spring, it's sure to add a clever touch to your decor.

Tool-Holder Bud Vase

Hardware meets science meets flower arranging in this unconventional composition. The metal base is a small hand-tool holder that locks onto pegboard. It's proven as an effective method for organizing your workshop, garage, or basement. In our design, however, it serves an altogether different purpose.

Pegboard comes in several types. We've selected a white plastic version to create a clean, minimal backdrop. You also could choose a tempered brown pegboard and leave it unfinished, or paint it anyway you wish. Once the board is prepared to your liking, simply insert the hooks of the tool holder into its holes. Since there are so many holes on the board, you can experiment with different levels and positions until you find the one that's right for you. (If you plan to wall-mount the pegboard, see page 97 for further instructions.)

A test tube is a common laboratory supply made from borosilicate glass for strength and heat resistance. You may have recently seen test tubes used more artfully to contain bath products or spices. They also make wonderful bud vases when you have single stems you wish to display.

Test tubes come in many diameters, but only two major categories: rimmed and unrimmed. Rimmed test tubes are the correct ones to use in this project as they have a protruding lip around their opening which will rest on top of the metal tool holder. (Unrimmed test tubes maintain the same diameter all the way up and will slide through the tool holder.) An 18 x 150-mm rimmed test tube, the standard lab issue, is also the perfect fit for our design. Just mount the tool holder, slide one test tube into each metal ring, add water, and insert some breathtaking blooms.

Washer Pillows

Hardware doesn't have to be hard. These comfortable cushions reveal the softer side of the home improvement center. Felt washers make fabulous pillow trim. Just arrange them any way you choose, and then attach them with a simple stitch. If you can't find felt washers, use self-adhesive felt furniture glides, which come in a variety of sizes and colors.

You Will Need

Felt-covered pillow*

Self-adhesive felt washers

Fabric marking pen or pencil

Pearl cotton thread

Needle

Scissors

Don't feel obligated to use only a felt-covered pillow. Any ready-made pillow will do. If you're handy with a needle and thread, you can sew a simple envelope-style pillow cover of your own.

1. Remove the cover from the pillow you have chosen. Lay it on a flat surface.

2. Play with the position of the felt washers. When you're happy with an arrangement, use the marking pen to mark their placement.

3. Cut several 5-inch (12.7 cm) lengths of the pearl cotton thread. Thread your needle with one thread.

4. Stitch the washers to the pillow cover as desired. For a decorative touch, we left the tails of the thread free rather than trimming them closely.

Carpenter Apron Carryall

Children might enjoy cleaning up their rooms when they can stuff their toys and treasures into this adorable hardware-inspired carryall. A portable tote with plenty of pockets, this clever soft storage organizer can be tied on a bed as shown, or you can take it along when you hit the road. Handy apron ties let you hang it up anywhere, such as behind a car seat or closet door.

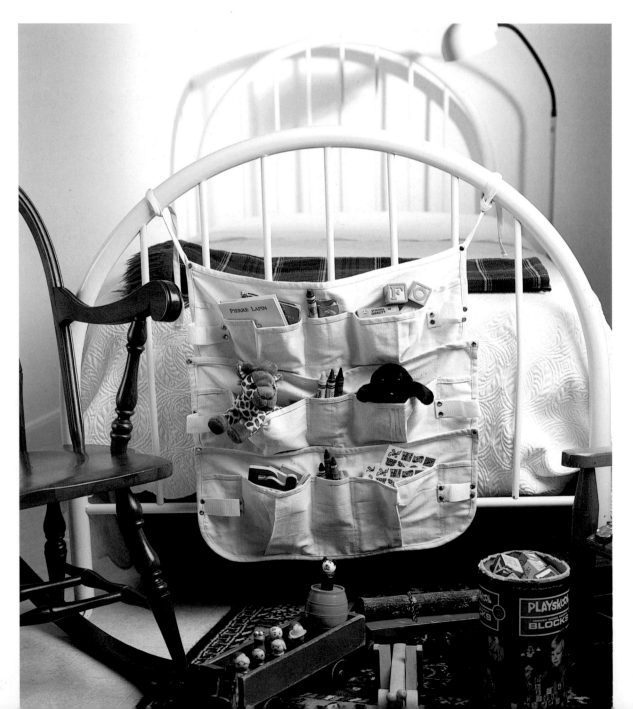

You Will Need

3 canvas carpenter aprons

Sewing machine or hand-sewing needle

Thread

1. Line up the bottom edge of one canvas carpenter apron with the top edge of a second apron. Machine- or hand-stitch the edges of the two aprons together.

2. Line up the top edge of the third apron with the bottom edge of the aprons sewn in step 1. Machine- or hand-stitch the third apron in place.

3. Cut off the carpenter apron strings from the bottom two aprons.

4. Tie both remaining strings on the top apron into secure hanging loops.

Every home improvement center carries at least a dozen hardware cabinets and tool chests to help professional carpenters and weekend do-it-yourselfers stay organized. These boxes run the gamut in size, price, and design. One of the most basic models is the plastic one shown. Although simple, this hardware cabinet has great features, such as clear drawers for easy viewing. All its hanging hardware is included, so mounting the cabinet to a wall or an interior cabinet door is a breeze. Most hardware cabinets even come with temporary labels you can customize and affix to the drawers. If you've ever desperately riffled through spice bottles, you'll know what a relief it would be to have clearly labeled drawers, all facing forward.

A hardware cabinet is also a practical storage system if you buy your spices in bulk or grow your own. Few fresh markets or grocery cooperatives carry prepackaged goods. This is an honorable effort to provide the most flavorful spices, but leaves you with anonymous plastic bags. After your shopping is finished, wouldn't it be a relief to come home and parcel out your spices into neatly arranged drawers? Just being able to see the colors so clearly may inspire you to new culinary heights.

Spiced-Up Hardware Cabinet

The kitchen is a hot spot. From cooking and eating to entertaining and working, more people are spending more time in what is often a small room. Any opportunity to gain space (and time) through creative, practical storage is important; any solution that's as good-looking as this spice rack is a double delight.

Wire-Brush Bouquet

Create this still-life masterpiece in metal, and you'll have an everlasting floral arrangement with no watering required (we're still working on the fragrance). Imitation flowers try to replicate blossoms; whereas this conceptual home center assemblage, based on an elbow vase, screen-door springs, and wire-wheel brushes, hinges on open minds and nimble imaginations.

You Will Need

Handsaw

Scrap wood pieces, 1-inch (2.5 cm) thick

Galvanized elbow, 8 inches (20.3 cm) tall

Sandpaper

Screwdriver

2 wood screws, 1 ½ inches (3.8 cm)

Spray paint, silver

Contact cement

5 wire-wheel brushes with stems, assorted diameters and metals

5 screen-door springs, each 15 inches (38.1 cm) long

Wire cutters

1. Use the handsaw to cut a 4 ½ x 4 ½-inch (11.4 x 11.4 cm) piece of the scrap wood. Cut out a wood circle, also from scrap, that fits inside the galvanized elbow. Sand the edges of both cut wood pieces.

2. Use the screwdriver and wood screws to attach the wood circle on top of the wood square.

3. Following the manufacturer's instructions and working in a well-ventilated area or outdoors, spray paint the wood silver. Let the paint completely dry between several thin, even coats.

4. Use the contact cement to glue the base of the galvanized elbow over the painted wood circle. (The bottom edge of the elbow sits on the top of the square.)

5. Push the stem of one wire-wheel brush into the opening at the end of one screen-door spring. Repeat with the rest of the brushes and springs.

6. Use the wire cutters to trim the bottom ends of the springs to create different heights for the wire-brush flowers. Arrange the flowers in the elbow vase.

Neat Cleat

Some hardware is too pretty to hide. Fortunately, there's no hard-and-fast rule that says you have to. Enter the rope cleat, a super-sleek and elegant fixture that instantly adds class and character to the pictures that grace your walls.

A rope cleat is a bi-level, long, and narrow piece of metal with slightly raised ends. It has screw holes in the center so it can be anchored to a wall. Cleats are commonly used to secure rope from flagpoles, window blinds, and boats. Most are zinc-plated for indoor and outdoor use. The larger models are easier to use, and, as you can see, make more of an impact.

You Will Need

Framed artwork with hanging wire

Rope cleat, ours is 4 ½ inches (11.4 cm) wide

Measuring tape

Drill with screwdriver bit

2 wood screws (if not sold with cleat)

2 plastic wall anchors (optional)

Drill bit (if using plastic anchors)

Grosgrain ribbon or other sturdy cord
(ours is 1 inch [2.5 cm] wide)

1. Determine where you'd like the framed artwork to hang. Make a small pencil mark on the wall at the top edge of the frame. Place the artwork aside.

2. With the frame resting on the floor or a table, hold the cleat above it and determine how much space you want between them. Measure the distance from the top of the frame to the screw holes in the cleat. Make a new mark on the wall above the one marked in step 1 based on this measurement.

3. Fasten the rope cleat to the wall at the point marked in step 3. (Use plastic wall anchors if you aren't screwing the cleat into a stud.)

4. Cut two generous lengths of the ribbon. On the back of the picture frame, tie one end of each ribbon to opposite sides of the hanging wire. Bring the artwork to the wall, and position the top edge of the frame on the mark made in step 1. Wrap the free ends of the ribbon around the cleat, tie a square knot for safety, and then tie a decorative bow.

Bold Bolts

When you have something special you wish to display, let your imagination and the irresistible resources of the hardware department inspire you. Wall-hung artwork doesn't always come with a wire on the back, nor does it always need one. This tile is secured to the wall with a stocky set of exposed hex bolts and washers. Under different circumstances, you could place the hardware along the top and bottom edges of the artwork instead of the top and side.

You Will Need

Artwork to be hung

Measuring tape

Drill with screwdriver bit

Small screw for pilot hole

4 plastic wall anchors to fit hex bolts

4 large flat washers

4 hex bolts, long enough to support artwork and securely fasten into wall

Pliers

1. Measure and mark the four places on the wall where the bolts will be inserted. It's a good idea to position the hardware approximately 1 inch (2.5 cm) or more in from the corners of the artwork.

2. Use the drill and the small screw to make pilot holes at all four marked locations. Insert one plastic wall anchor into each pilot hole.

3. Place one large flat washer on each hex bolt. One at a time, guide the bolts into the plastic wall anchors, leaving enough room to slide the artwork behind the washers.

4. Once the artwork is in place, gently tighten the bolts with pliers to secure, but not damage, the piece. Repeat steps 1 through 4 to install as many pieces of art as you wish.

Spring Towel Loop

A spring may be the most flexible piece of
hardware. This inherent versatility is as good
as gold to the hardware style designer. Bend,
twist, or even knot a spring into the shape
you desire, and you're well on your way to
creating an expressive home accent. Coiled
wire, the root of all springs, is sold in various
gauges and diameters. An especially stout
type inspired the designer to concoct this
inviting towel loop.

You Will Need

Pliers

Spring, 14 inches (35.6 cm),
1 ½-inch (3.8 cm) diameter

Double hook hanger

Screwdriver or drill

1. Use the pliers to slightly open one end of
the spring.

2. Curve the ends of the spring to meet. Hook the
open end into the one that is closed.

3. Using the screwdriver or drill, attach the
double-hook hanger to the wall with the hardware provided by the manufacturer.

4. Place each spring end over one hook on the
double hanger.

six ways to find a stud

For optimum security and strength, always attempt to use studs to support wall-hung objects, such as shelves, artwork, and even towel bars. Studs form the backbone of your home. They are the vertical system of wood or metal framing hidden behind finished walls.

There are many ways to locate the studs behind your walls. Although no single approach is 100-percent guaranteed, if you apply one or more of the following techniques, you can locate studs without too much trouble. Once you find one stud, locating others is fairly easy. Studs, measured from center to center, are usually spaced 16 or 24 inches (40.6 or 61 cm) apart.

1. *Use an electronic stud finder*. This is a quick and reliable method that works on all types of walls. An electronic stud finder detects changes in density. Just pass it over your wall, and a light, display, or tone lets you know when it's over a stud.

2. *Use a magnetic stud finder*. This easy-to-use tool locates the fasteners that attach drywall to studs. Slide the stud finder over the wall, and its magnetized bar will point to screws, nails, or metallic studs. Unfortunately, they also point to everything else metal that lies behind your wall, such as pipes, cable, and nails and screws that may be far from studs.

3. *Inspect your baseboards and crown moldings for nails or nail holes*. These are frequently attached to studs. Also, outlet boxes for light switches or receptacles are usually mounted to one side of a stud.

4. *Shine a light along a wall at a flat angle and look for depressions and seams*. Slight dimples can indicate the position where nails or screws fasten drywall to studs. Long vertical seams can show where drywall panel edges meet on a stud.

5. *Rap along the wall with your knuckles or with a hammerhead wrapped in a soft towel*. This is a popular, though somewhat unreliable, method. If you listen closely, you may be able to distinguish a slightly higher sound over studs and a hollow sound elsewhere.

6. *Insert a bent wire clothes hanger into the wall after drilling a hole and missing a stud*. Spin the wire to the left and right behind the wall until it hits a stud.

Wine Stoppers

Give your wine bottles a taste of hardware style by adorning their corks with fancy home-center gadgets. These stoppers help you guide the corks and bring fashion to your table. From a designer cabinet pull to an industrial shut-off valve, anything will work, even items without a built-in stem.

Cabinet or Drawer Pull

You Will Need

Cabinet or drawer pull with bolt to fit

Wire cutters

Wine bottle cork

1. Screw the bolt into the drawer or cabinet pull.

2. Use the wire cutters to cut off the bold head.

3. Screw the bolt into the top of the wine bottle cork.

Sillcock Handle

You Will Need

Bolt, 1 ½ inches (3.8 cm)

Sillcock handle, 1 ¾ inches (4.4 cm)

Hex nut

Wine bottle cork

1. Thread the 1 ½-inch (3.8 cm) bolt through the top hole of the sillcock handle.

2. Tightly screw the hex nut onto the 1 ½-inch (3.8 cm) bolt.

3. Screw the bolt into the top of the wine bottle cork.

Brass Replacement Ball

You Will Need

Headless screw

Brass replacement ball (an interior fitting for a single-handle faucet, found with plumbing supplies)

Wine bottle cork

1. Screw the headless screw into the bottom of the brass replacement ball.

2. Attach the opposite end of the screw into the top of the wine bottle cork.

Sillcock Key

You Will Need

Wire cutters

Bolt, 2 inches (5 cm)

Sillcock key

2 hex nuts

Wine bottle cork

1. Use the wire cutters to clip off the head of the 2-inch (5 cm) bolt.

2. Thread the headless 2-inch (5 cm) bolt through the sillcock key.

3. Screw one hex nut at the top of the bolt. Screw the second hex nut at the bottom of the bolt and tighten.

4. Screw the sillcock key into the cork.

What's a Sillcock Handle & Key?

A sillcock is an outdoor water faucet. It's typically located just above a building's *sill*, the board fastened to the top of the foundation, hence the name. A sillcock handle is the knob you use to control the water flow from this faucet. A sillcock key is used in place of a sillcock handle for faucets that need to be protected from widespread use, such as those attached to public buildings.

Expanded Cable

Cable is multiple strands of wire woven together to form a single strong line. Perhaps you've seen lengths of cable suspending light fixtures or running along stair rails. Cable doesn't stretch, is generally more sturdy than rope, and looks incredibly chic. Its modern, upscale appearance enhances any design. Even a simple message center line benefits from a cable makeover.

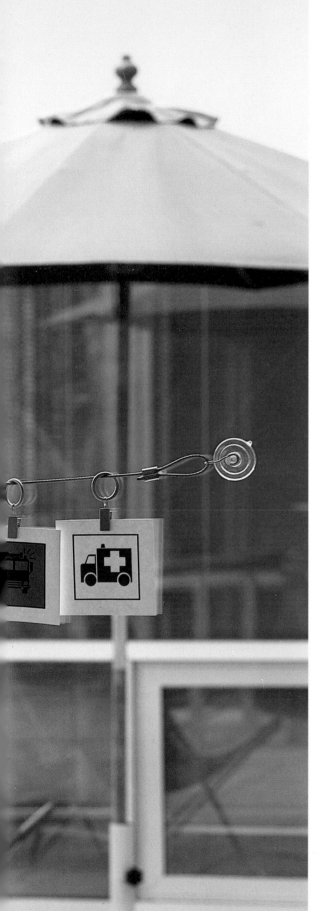

You Will Need

Cable, ⅛ inch (3 mm) wide*

2 aluminum ferrules (also known as cable crimps or stops), ⅛ inch (3 mm)

Swaging tool (you could use a hammer instead; this application is more decorative than it is weight-bearing)

Curtain or shower curtain rod clips, as many as desired

2 suction-cup hooks

*Most home improvement centers store cable on reels and cut it to your order. Determine how long you want your message line to be and add at least 6 inches (15.2 cm), so you can form the two end loops. Round this measurement up to the nearest foot. You always can cut off excess cable with a small bolt cutter or sharp wire cutters.

1. Feed one end of the cable through a hole on one ferrule. Pull out the end of the cable approximately 6 inches (15.2 cm); bend the cable; and feed the end through the second, empty hole in the ferrule to form a loop.

2. Use the swaging tool (or hammer) to secure the ferrule to the looped cable. If using a hammer, you only need to hit the ferrule two or three times. Hammer gently to avoid leaving marks on the metal.

3. String the curtain or shower curtain rod clips onto the cable.

4. Repeat steps 1 and 2 to create and secure a second loop on the cable at the opposite end.

5. Attach the suction-cup hooks to a window or other appropriate surface (see suction-cup manufacturer's recommendations). Hook one cable loop over each hook. Adjust the hooks as necessary so the cable becomes taut. Spread the rod clips apart, and hang anything you desire.

What's a Cable Ferrule?
A free end of cable is fed through two holes in this oblong metal clip to form a loop. The holes in the ferrule are then compressed to prevent the cable from slipping. A ferrule also prevents cut cable ends from fraying into loose strands of wire.

What's a Swaging Tool?
A swaging tool crimps cable ferrules up to ⅛ inch (3 mm) in diameter. Similar in appearance to a bolt cutter, this hand tool has forged jaws for increased strength and provides great leverage.

Toolbox Table

If diamonds are a girl's best friend, then diamond-plate metal toolboxes are the crown jewels of the home improvement center. Poised on their aisle, dignified and gleaming, these boxes are irresistible. Thanks to our talented designer, they're not just for tools anymore. Fashion a simple metal pipe stand, set a diamond-plate toolbox on top, stash your remote controls, books, or knitting inside, and you've got an end table that's a real gem.

You Will Need

Diamond-plate aluminum toolbox, 9 x 24 x 9 ¾ inches (22.9 x 60.9 x 24.8 cm), with detached handle and handle-mounting hardware

Epoxy putty, gray

Drill

Drill bit, slightly smaller diameter than handle screws

Silver paint

Small paintbrush

Manual pipe cutter

Electrical pipe, 20 feet (6.1 m) long, ½-inch (1.3 cm) diameter

Steel wool

8 galvanized tees, ½-inch (1.3 cm) diameter

8 galvanized corners, ½-inch (1.3 cm) diameter

Contact cement

Metal screws, optional

1. If there are holes on the top of the toolbox where the handle would be attached, fill them in with the gray epoxy putty. Let the epoxy putty dry for the amount of time its manufacturer recommends.

2. Decide where you'd like to position the toolbox handle on the front side of the toolbox. Mark this location, and then drill holes for the handle. Attach the handle to the front of the toolbox with the hardware provided.

3. Use the silver paint and the small brush to paint over the gray epoxy putty to match the toolbox.

4. Use the manual pipe cutter to cut four pieces of the electrical pipe, each 22 inches (55.9 cm) long. Cut four more pieces of pipe, each 15 inches (38.1 cm) long, and then four more pieces of pipe, each 8 inches (20.3 cm) long. Clean the electrical pipe pieces with the steel wool to remove any writing.

5. To construct the table frame, place a galvanized tee on both ends of each 8-inch (20.3 cm) piece of cut pipe. Position two 22-inch (55.9 cm) pieces of pipe parallel to each other. Place two of the 8-inch pipes between the 22-inch pipes. Connect the 22-inch (side) pipes to the 8-inch (end) pipes with the galvanized corners. Repeat this step with a second set of pipes.

6. Adjust the tees on the end pipes so their openings face each other. Place the 15-inch (38.1 cm) pipe pieces into the tees. Use the contact cement to glue all the pipes and connectors together. Let the contact cement dry for the amount of time its manufacturer recommends.

7. Attach the diamond-plate toolbox to the top of the table frame with metal screws or epoxy putty if you wish, or simply leave it as a separate, portable unit.

dress it up with hardware

Nothing ordinary has to stay that way long, especially when you have a whole home improvement center full of embellishment ideas from which to choose. To prove this point, we spruced up three plain objects, each in under an hour, with splended results.

Spacers & Studs

You Will Need

Broad-faced wood frame

Paint and paintbrush (optional)

Ceramic-tile spacers

Cyanoacrylate glue

Upholstery tacks

Hammer

1. If desired (or if the wood is unfinished), paint the frame. Let dry.

2. Arrange the tile spacers on the frame. Re-arrange them. Play with their placement until you're satisfied with the design.

3. Use the cyanoacrylate glue to adhere the spacers to the frame. Let the glue dry.

4. Accent each spacer with an upholstery tack. Use the hammer, if needed, to drive each tack into the center of the spacer.

What's a Ceramic-tile Spacer?
Besides being phenomenally cute, these tiny plastic crosses are absolutely necessary for properly laying tile. They speed up the arranging process and keep an even distance between tiles prior to applying grout. Tile spacers range in thickness from $\frac{1}{16}$ to $\frac{3}{8}$ inch (1.6 to 9.5 mm), are less than 1 inch (2.5 cm) across, and are sold in bags of up to 300 pieces, so you'll have plenty with which to work.

Debonair Debris

You Will Need

Fine-gauge copper wire

Wire cutters or scissors

Copper washers

Metal mesh wastebasket

Pliers

1. Cut several short lengths of copper wire, each approximately 2 to 3 inches (5 to 7.6 cm) long. Set them aside.

2. Use one length of wire to attach a copper washer to the mesh wastebasket. Feed the wire ends through the metal mesh, and then use pliers to twist the wire tightly together on the interior of the basket.

3. Repeat step 2 to wire the rest of the washers on the basket randomly or in a pattern.

4. Use wire cutters or scissors to closely trim the ends of the twisted wires inside the basket.

Dotty Shade

You Will Need

Rubber washers in a variety of sizes

Lamp with undecorated shade

Cyanoacrylate glue

Glue the rubber washers to the lampshade in any configuration you can imagine; screw a lightbulb into the lamp, plug it in, turn it on, and bask in the glow of your accomplishment!

Storage & Organization Department

Home improvement centers are chock-full of the boxes, rods, buckets, and hangers that help to simplify life through efficient storage and organization. From substantial furniture pieces, such as utility cabinets, to tiny helpful hooks, the storage and organization aisles at today's hardware store are surprisingly well-stocked. These products, made from a vast range of materials, such as wood, plastic, metal, cork, and laminate, are practical, easy solutions for containing some of life's clutter. With only slight modifications, you can convert these functional (yet often visually dull) items into eye-catching accents for your home decor.

Hooks

Handy hooks are a simple form of open storage. They can be used in the bathroom, closet, or kitchen, to help you keep often-used items sorted and within reach. Whether you need a single-, double-, or multiple-hook unit, you can find what you're looking for at any home improvement center. From ordinary to ornate, there is a hook shape for every taste, decor, and budget. In addition to the permanent types that attach to the wall, there are also new models designed to be mobile. Over-the-door hooks and hangers have become quite popular, as have suction and adhesive-backed hooks.

Hangers

Under traditional circumstances, most hangers serve a less decorative, more utilitarian role. They are designed to fulfill a specific need, such as storing a bicycle, a ladder, or a garden hose. Multihanger units can also hold hand tools, mops, and brooms. Because their weight-bearing capacity is generally greater, hangers are often used to organize workshops, garages, and sheds. Although their decorative potential is less obvious, hangers can be just the right accessory in a hardware-savvy home.

Boxes, Buckets, Tubs & Totes

Plastic reigns supreme here. The home center aisles are filled with every size and shape of container imaginable to make your projects easier and life more organized. Some products have lids, some have handles, some stack, and some even come on wheels—the array is almost dizzying. From a bright plastic bucket to a hinged trunk, there's a container just begging to be customized into a unique home accent.

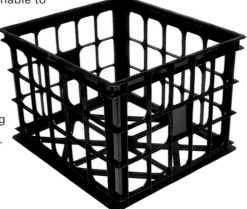

Multipurpose Storage Units

Whether you need a freestanding or a mountable cabinet, one with a single door or multiple drawers, finished or unfinished, you're sure to find just the configuration you're looking for at the home improvement center. These units come in all shapes and sizes and most require assembly. Many multipurpose storage units come with adjustable shelves, making them even easier to customize. Just add a decorative paint motif, a set of casters, or some hardware accessories, and you've got a trendy, one-of-a-kind piece.

Sundries

Every respectable hardware store, large or small, has a corner devoted to *sundries*, miscellaneous yet indispensable merchandise that defies categorization. Old-fashioned sundries, such as wooden hangers or a clothes-drying rack, are still around as well as newer products (ones we never knew we needed but now can't live without), such as a non-skid shelf liner or a dry-erase message board.

Flower Power

Every room is enhanced by the unsurpassed beauty of flowers. You might think that to create a striking and memorable arrangement takes a lot of time, money, and training, yet some of the most effective presentations are often the most simple. These four oil cans, each displaying a single bloom, are a quick and delightfully easy way to add flower power.

You can accomplish this decoration by simply purchasing the oil cans, filling them with water, and inserting the flowers of your choice. Alternately, you can cut off the tips of the spouts to different heights as shown. Use a hacksaw, grinder, or jigsaw with a metal blade to trim the spout, and then smooth away any rough edges with a metal file. Cutting off the spout tops also increases the diameter of the holes. This allows the oil-can vases to hold flowers with larger stems.

Our designer found these brilliant blue oil cans at the hardware store. She loves using them to inject a bold dash of color on a glass tabletop. If you can't locate colored oil cans or you desire a more subdued palette, feel free to paint the metal any color under the sun.

Sideways Bucket Cubbies

When ambling through the home improvement center searching for inspiration, it's important to consider the merchandise from all angles. As this project clearly indicates, galvanized buckets can be just as practical and attractive sideways as they are in their normal upright position. No complex metal skills are needed to construct this multipurpose shelving unit. Simply bolt the buckets together, hang them up, and fill them with towels, magazines, or whatever you wish to store.

You Will Need

3 large paint buckets with handles

2 small paint buckets with handles

Drill and metal drill bit

7 bolts, ½ inch (1.3 cm)

7 hex nuts to fit bolts

Hammer and nail

Wall screws

1. Arrange the buckets in the layout you desire.

2. At the point where the bucket sides meet, drill through both metal surfaces.

3. Run the bolts through the drilled holes, and then screw on the hex nuts.

4. From the back side of the unit, use the hammer and nail to make a hole in the center of at least two buckets. Drive a screw through each of these two holes to attach the shelf to the wall.

Raise the Bar

Whether you're short on storage space or simply want to create a fanciful display, using a commercial bath towel bar with suitably sized S hooks or plant hangers may be the answer. Home improvement centers feature a wide selection of decorative kitchen and bath accessories. Among their stock are bath towel bars in metal, wood, ceramic, and plastic—all sold with mounting hardware, making installation a breeze. Today's towel bars are an appealing marriage of form and function, and, for the ambitious decorator, opportunities to use them are abundant.

You often see pots and pans hung on a decorative kitchen rack to keep them neatly organized and easy to reach. Why not install a similar, smaller system for mugs? Even if you're not a morning person, you'll know exactly where to reach for that all-important first cup of coffee or tea. All mugs have a handle which easily and securely fits over any type of hook. A set of matching white mugs lined up in a row is a vision of pure simplicity (see photo, left). This method also works well if your mugs are an eclectic mix of shape and style. A visible assortment of handmade ceramics, production pottery, or even collectible restaurant china will liven up any setting and make a strong impression.

The second arrangement travels farther from convention and uses the towel-bar system to display a series of matted and framed photographs (see photo, below). The idea is modest yet extremely effective. The wire on the back of each picture is hung over a single hook. (You may wish to use two hooks per photo if the artworks are large or to keep them level.) By sliding the hooks along the bar the photos can be spread apart or grouped together as you wish without making additional nail holes in your wall.

Towel bars and hooks have many other interesting applications around the home. Mount a short bar for utensils, and you'll never have to dig through overcrowded drawers to find your whisk. You know grandmother's beaded handbags boxed up in the attic, or her dashing feathered hats and scarves? Why not hang them up on a towel bar for a splash of romantic color? Towel bars also make great magazine and newspaper holders.

Magnetic Messages

Why would you settle for a boring cork bulletin board when there's a world of colors and textures from which to choose? This design features the bumpy surface of an anti-skid shelf liner in a cheery bright red. It's paired with smooth aluminum flashing for visual contrast. (Galvanizing causes the aluminum to become magnetized.) Unlike most message boards, this one's reversible—the back side is a blackboard for communiques in chalk.

You Will Need

Framed blackboard, 17 x 23 inches (43.2 x 58.4 cm)

Galvanized aluminum flashing, 10 inches (25.4 cm) wide

Red anti-skid shelf liner

Cork board, 12 x 15 inches (30.5 x 38.1 cm)

Spray adhesive

Contact cement

Drill and drill bit or hammer and small nail

5 hooks, each 2 inches (5 cm)

2 eye hooks

Thin metal cable, 36 inches (.9 m)

2 wire crimps to fit cable

Pliers

1. Measure the height of the back side of the blackboard, not including the frame. Cut a piece of the 10-inch-wide (25.4 cm) galvanized flashing to this measurement.

2. Use the contact cement to glue the flashing to the left side of the back of the blackboard.

3. Measure and cut a 12 ½ x 15 ½-inch (31.8 x 39.4 cm) piece of the shelf liner. Use the spray adhesive to adhere the cork board to the shelf liner. Center the cork on top of the liner. Wrap the excess liner around the edges of the cork. Let the adhesive dry.

4. Use the contact cement to affix the back of the wrapped cork board to the right side of the back of the blackboard. Let dry.

5. Mark five evenly spaced points along the bottom edge of the blackboard frame. Make pilot holes in the frame at these points with the drill or with a hammer and small nail. Screw the hooks into the bottom edge of the blackboard frame.

6. Mark two points on the top edge of the blackboard frame for the eye hooks. Make pilot holes at these points, and then screw in the hooks.

7. Feed the thin cable through each eye hook, place a crimp on the cable at each end, and then use the pliers to secure the crimp onto the cable.

What's Flashing?

Flashing is a flexible and very thin (.01 inch [.2 mm]) sheet metal used to weatherproof and reinforce roofs. It's a soft material that shapes easily and holds form well. Typically, flashing is aluminum, but it can also be copper, steel, and zinc. Variations are manufactured with either a mill (uncoated), galvanized (zinc-coated), or painted finish. Flashing is conveniently sold on rolls of various widths and lengths in the building materials department of home improvement centers.

You Will Need

Undecorated white cabinet

Assorted tools to trace

Pencil

Paint pens

Casters with mounting hardware (optional)

1. Lay the undecorated cabinet flat on the floor. (This makes tracing the tools much easier than attempting to trace them vertically.)

2. Use a pencil to trace around the contour of one tool, and then repeat with different tools. Place the tools on different cabinet surfaces. If the cabinet has many drawers, you could organize your tools by decorating each drawer with the appropriate tool outline.

3. Use paint pens in the color or colors of your choice to outline and detail each tool.

4. Add casters to your cabinet if desired.

High-Profile Chest

You don't need special drawing skills to adorn a cabinet with these foolproof tool designs. Just trace the silhouettes of tools, and then color over their outlines with paint pens. What could be easier? Add locking casters to your one-of-a-kind cabinet so you can conveniently wheel it from project to project.

Half-a-Hanger Hook Board

Turn home decor upside down with this surreal twist. Inverted clothes hangers hold jeans and things just as well as more traditional hooks. Use a precut shelf as the backing board to save time and effort. The results are mesmerizing.

You Will Need

Pine shelf board, 9 ½ x 34 x 1 inch (24.1 x 86.4 x 2.5 cm)

Sandpaper

Polyurethane spray, semi-gloss

5 wooden clothes hangers

Handsaw

Drill and drill bit

15 wood screws, 1 ¼ inches (3.2 cm)

Screwdriver

3 eye hooks

1. Sand the front face, ends, and edges of the pine shelf board, and then clean off all sawdust and debris.

2. Following the manufacturer's instructions, spray two or three coats of polyurethane on the shelf board. Let dry.

3. On both the hanger bar and the dowel of all five wood hangers, measure and mark a line ½ inch (1.3 cm) off the center point on the same side of the hook. Use the handsaw to cut the hangers at this point.

4. Find the horizontal center of the shelf board. Place one of the half-hangers on the center line.

5. Adjust the height of the hanger so the metal hook hangs below the shelf. Trace the outline of the hanger bar and the dowel onto the wood shelf.

6. Make two small marks under the traced hanger bar and one small mark under the traced dowel. Drill small holes at these three marks.

7. From the back side of the shelf board, place a screw into each hole. Use the screwdriver to drive the screws in until they just come through the front of the shelf.

8. Place the hanger back on the front of the shelf. Firmly press the screw tips into the cut ends of the rod and dowel. Drill the hanger at the three marks made by the screw tips. Position the hanger back on the shelf, and screw it in place.

9. Measure 7 inches (17.8 cm) to the left of the first attached hanger, and repeat steps 5 through 8.

10. Measure 7 inches (17.8 cm) to the left of the hanger attached in step 9, and repeat steps 5 through 8.

11. Repeat steps 9 and 10 on the right side of the center hanger.

12. Drill a pilot hole at the center point on the top edge of the shelf. Screw in an eye hook. Attach another eye hook 14 inches (35.6 cm) to the left, and then 14 inches (35.6 cm) to the right of the center eye hook.

drilling tips

Compared to the old-style brace and auger bit, making holes with an electric drill is easy. Here are a few good drilling tips, so your holes will be round, straight, and properly angled.

• Drill bits often stray from the marked spots, making it hard to start a hole. To keep the bit from sliding around, create a small dimple with a center punch before drilling. (A *center punch* can be any kind of tool with a point on one end and a flat surface to hammer on the other.)

• If you plan to drill large-diameter holes, first make a smaller hole, and then enlarge it incrementally to its final size.

• Clamp down the wood or metal to be drilled, or place a backing board under the surface. (Using a backing board also helps to make clean holes on both sides of the surface you're drilling.)

• To drill a perpendicular hole without the luxury of a drill press, line up the shank of the bit with the edge of a framing square or use a drill with a built-in spirit level.

Tufted Headboard

Create a distinctive focal point for the bedroom by transforming an ordinary painter's drop cloth into a luxurious headboard. Generous layers of foam and batting stuffed behind the canvas give the board plenty of cushion. Instead of using traditional methods, the designer puckered the fabric surface with elegant drawer pulls straight from the hardware aisle.

You Will Need

Spray adhesive

Foam, 2 ½ x 5 ½ feet (.76 x 1.7 m), 1 inch (2.5 cm) thick

Plywood, 2 ½ x 5 ½ feet (.76 x 1.7 m)

Batting, 2 yards (1.8 m)

Staple gun and staples

Canvas drop cloth, 6 x 9 feet (1.8 x 2.7 m)

Drill and drill bit

Ice pick

6 drawer pulls of your choice

Screwdriver

1. Use the spray adhesive to adhere the 1-inch-thick (2.5 cm) foam onto the plywood.

2. Spread the batting out on the floor. Place the plywood and foam piece on top of the batting with the foam side down. Pull the batting around the foam and plywood. Use the staple gun to attach the batting to the back side of the plywood at 6-inch (15.2 cm) intervals.

3. Cut the canvas drop cloth to a 3 ½ x 6-foot (1.1 x 1.8 m) rectangle. In a clean area, spread the canvas out on the floor. Place the plywood, batting side down, on top of the canvas.

4. At the center of each edge, pull the canvas to the back side of the plywood, and staple it in place with the staple gun. Tightly pull the canvas, and staple it down all the way around the board, carefully folding the fabric at the corners.

5. Draw a horizontal line across the back side of the plywood, 8 inches (20.3 cm) down from its top edge. Locate and mark the center of this line. Mark a point on the line 15 inches (38.1 cm) to the right of the center point; then mark a point on the line 15 inches (38.1 cm) to the left of center. Measure 8 ½ inches (21.6 cm) straight down from these three marks (left, right, and center), and make three more marks at these points. (You now have a total of six marks.)

6. Drill each mark from the back side of the plywood, making sure not to let the drill twist into the foam and batting. From the back side of the plywood, use the ice pick to poke a hole through the foam, batting, and canvas.

7. From the back side of the plywood, thread the drawer-pull screws through the wood to the canvas. On the front side of the headboard, attach the drawer pulls to the screws. (If the drawer-pull screws are too long, put hex nuts onto the screws before inserting them into the plywood.)

place mat matters

When you fashion a set of place mats from the home center aisles, you'll have a table setting that's undeniably unique and virtually hassle free. By using interesting and durable materials, such as rubber, metal, and plastic mesh, you'll bring great design to the table and eliminate the task of laundering and ironing (even dry cleaning) linens. Each set of instructions is for a single mat; simply repeat the steps to make more.

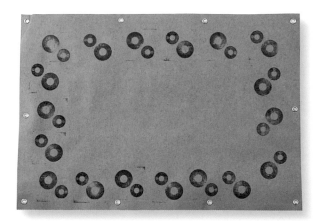

Target Practice

You Will Need
Contractor's paper

Spray adhesive

Hole punch

Eyelets and eyelet punch

Rubber washers

Small wood block

Glue

Rubber stamp ink

Acrylic varnish (optional)

1. Determine what size place mats you wish to make. Measure and cut three rectangles to this size from the roll of contractor's paper.

2. Use the spray adhesive to glue the three sheets of contractor's paper together in an orderly stack.

3. Use the hole punch to make evenly spaced holes around the edges of the multi-layer paper rectangle.

4. Set the eyelets into the holes with the eyelet punch.

5. To create the rubber stamp, glue the rubber washers to the small wood block.

6. Decorate the place mat as desired with the rubber stamp and ink. Let the ink dry.

7. Finish the paper place mats with a coat of acrylic varnish if you wish to extend the length of their service.

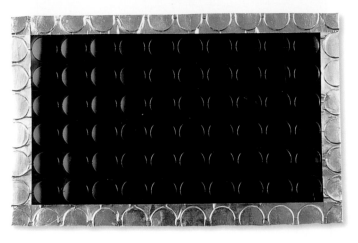

Foiled Again

Private Screening

You Will Need
Fiberglass screening

Straight pins

Sewing machine

Thread, color of your choice

1. Determine what size place mats you wish to make. Measure and cut out three rectangles of the desired size from the roll of fiberglass screening.

2. Evenly stack the three rectangles on top of each other, and pin them together with straight pins.

3. Set the sewing machine on an ornamental stitch (we used a zigzag). Stitch one or more decorative rows around the edges of the place mat to hold all three layers together.

You Will Need
Molded vinyl black floor runner, raised circle design

Silver foil tape, 2 inches (5 cm) wide

Wood craft stick

1. Measure and mark the molded vinyl black floor runner into an 11 x 18-inch (27.9 x 45.7 cm) rectangle. Cut out this form with scissors.

2. Cut two pieces of the silver foil tape, each 18 inches (45.7 cm) in length. Cut two more pieces of the tape, each 11 inches (27.9 cm) long.

3. Carefully remove the backing strip from one of the 11-inch (27.9 cm) pieces of silver foil tape. Place the edge of the tape on the front and short side of the black vinyl mat, 1 inch (2.5 cm) in from its edge. Turn the mat over, and wrap the remaining tape onto the back side of the mat. Lightly rub the tape down.

4. With the front side of the mat facing up, use a wood craft stick to gently rub the foil tape into place, exposing the contour of the molded vinyl under the tape.

5. Repeat steps 3 and 4 on the remaining edges of the mat with the appropriately sized tape strips.

Woven Veneer

You Will Need

Solid shelf liner, taupe or color of your choice

Wood veneer edging

Oak stain

Paintbrush

Polyurethane spray, semi-gloss

Hot-glue gun and hot glue

1. Measure and cut a 12 x 16-inch (30.5 x 40.6 cm) piece of the shelf liner.

2. Cut five strips of the wood veneer edging, each 16 inches (40.6 cm) long. Cut five more strips of the wood veneer edging, each 12 inches (30.5 cm) long.

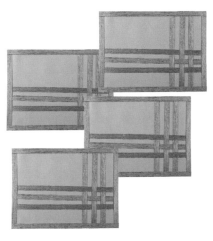

3. Following the manufacturer's instructions, stain the wood veneer edging with the oak-colored stain. Let dry.

4. Apply several thin and even coats of the polyurethane spray to all 10 strips of stained veneer until you achieve the desired finish. Let dry.

5. Place the three long strips of wood veneer horizontally on top of the shelf liner. Place the three shorter strips on the shelf liner vertically. Weave the strips together in a simple over-and-under pattern.

6. Once the woven edging is in position, secure it to the shelf liner with a hot-glue gun and hot glue.

7. Hot-glue the remaining 12-inch (30.5 cm) veneer strips onto each vertical edge of the place mat. Hot-glue the remaining 16-inch (40.6 cm) veneer pieces onto each horizonal edge of the place mat.

Dashing Flashing

You Will Need

Aluminum flashing

Hot-glue gun and hot glue

1. Measure, mark, and cut out nine strips of the aluminum flashing, each 1 x 14 inches (2.5 x 35.6 cm). Cut 13 more strips of aluminum flashing, each 1 x 10 inches (2.5 x 25.4 cm).

2. Using a simple over-and-under technique, weave all the flashing strips together without gluing. (The long strips are the horizontal elements of the mat; run the shorter strips vertically.) Once woven, adjust the strips until they are evenly spaced.

3. On all four edges of the place mat, adhere the ends of the flashing strips by lifting them up one at a time and dabbing hot glue between them. If needed, use scissors to cut all the edges of the place mat square and even.

Plumbing Department

Plumbing may sound like the most unsavory department in the hardware store, yet when it comes to interesting home decor supplies, you'd be hard-pressed to find a better stash. Take supply pipe, for example. It can do a lot more than deliver water. With its convenient sizes and abundance of fittings, pipe is terrific for constructing everything from curtain rods to candelabras. Once you check out the plumbing aisles, you may feel more creative inspiration than ever.

Pipe & Pipe Fittings

Copper, cast iron, plastic, galvanized, black, brass—the variety of pipes and the number of their attendant fittings is astonishing. Fortunately, you'll be decorating with them and not actually plumbing!

Pipe sections are connected with *fittings*. These fittings allow pipes to be joined in a line, at an angle, or in a curve. There are three basic categories of pipe fittings. The first includes fittings designed for making bends and turns in the pipe. The second category has fittings made for joining together or branching multiple pipes. Even ones of different diameters. The final category includes couplings, adapters, and other means to join pipes, even ones with different diameters. This flexibility, matched by a distinct visual appeal, makes pipe an easy choice for many hardware-inspired home decor projects.

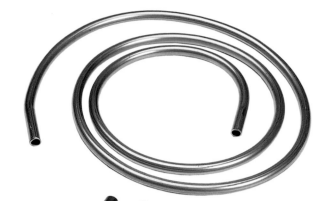

Copper Pipe & Tubing

Modern plumbing almost exclusively uses copper pipes for water feeds and central heating. Rigid copper pipe comes in diameters ranging from ⅛ to 12 inches (.3 to 30.5 cm). The three major categories ofcopper pipe are based on wall thickness: type K is thick; type L is medium; and type M is thin. Most home improvement centers stock copper pipes in 10-foot (3 m) lengths which you can easily cut to size at home (see page 55, Cutting Copper Pipe).

Galvanized Steel

These handsome gray pipes are created from zinc-treated steel. *Galvanization*, the coating of steel with zinc, makes the pipe rustproof. The longest galvanized steel pipes are sold in 21-foot (6.4 m) lengths, which most home improvement stores will cut to order. Shorter precut lengths are also sold in increments of 6 inches (15.2 cm) up to 6 feet (1.8 m). These pieces are usually threaded on both ends and range in diameter from ⅛ to 6 inches (.3 to 15.2 cm).

Other Pipe Options

Black iron pipe is often seamless and slightly greasy to the touch. This variety is similar to galvanized steel pipe, but it has not been zinc-treated for rust resistance. Without the galvanized finish, it cannot be used for water; instead it is used for steam and gas. Plastic pipes are plentiful. Their names usually have a chemical origin, *polyvinyl chloride pipe* for example, so they're commonly known by an acronym, in this case, *PVC*. Plastic pipes can perform all the functions of metal pipes and are often used inside and outside the home. Brass pipe is sold in all standard sizes and in various weights and lengths. It is much more expensive than other pipes and rarely used in home plumbing.

Flexing Candelabra

With its muscular stance and clean lines, this pipe candelabra is both handsome and refined. Who would have thought such an impression could be made by the joining of common plumbing parts? Add three lean and smooth colored candles and let your hardware style shine.

You Will Need

Galvanized steel pipe nipple, ¾ x 4 ½ inches (1.9 x 11.4 cm)

Galvanized steel floor flange, ¾ inch (1.9 cm)

Galvanized steel tee, ¾ inch (1.9 cm)

2 galvanized steel 90-degree elbows, ¾ inch (1.9 cm)

Galvanized steel cup, ¾ inch (1.9 cm)

Grey epoxy putty

1. Tightly screw one end of the pipe nipple into the floor flange.

2. Completely thread the bottom of the galvanized steel tee into the top of the pipe nipple.

3. Screw one 90-degree elbow into each side of the galvanized steel tee.

4. Following the manufacturer's instructions, use the gray epoxy putty to adhere the galvanized cap to the center of the tee.

Flower Grids

No one likes to find their fresh-cut flowers suddenly slumping over the sides of a vase. Florists use florist's tape or invisible tape to create a convenient grid across the mouth of a vase for stem support, but we've discovered a more attractive hardware-inspired system for keeping blooms at attention.

The elegant yellow daylily composition (above, left) features a polished brass strainer, 4 ½ inches (11.4 cm) in diameter. Conventionally used as a replacement part for shower drains, this strainer also fits nicely on top of a clear glass vase. Slim lily stems slide right through the strainer holes and are well supported by the grid.

To create the grid for the red daisy arrangement (above, right), use tin snips to cut out a square piece of hardware cloth larger than the mouth of the vase. (*Hardware cloth* is a heavily galvanized, firm, and non-raveling steel mesh.) Place the hardware cloth on the vase opening. Its edges can be parallel or turned at an angle as shown. Insert any flowers you like through the gaps in the grid.

Just because a suitcase stand is a classic concept doesn't mean it has to look dated. The moment we laid eyes on this delightfully industrial interpretation, we were convinced that there was no element of home decor that couldn't be improved by the home-center touch. Copper pipes are inexpensive and easy to cut and join. Once you start realizing their potential, you may find even more surprising uses.

You Will Need

Pipe cutter

2 pieces copper pipe, each 10 feet (3 m) long, ½-inch (1.3 cm) diameter

Drill and drill bit

2 bolts, 2 inches (5 cm)

2 hex nuts to fit bolts

2 cap nuts

8 copper corners, ½ inch (1.3 cm)

Contact cement

Woven jute, 5 yards (4.6 m) x 3 ½ inches (8.9 cm)

Sewing machine (optional)

Hand-sewing needle

Thread to match woven jute

Copper Suitcase Stand

1. Use the pipe cutter to cut four pieces of the copper pipe, each 31 inches (78.7 cm) long. Cut four more pieces of the copper pipe, each 20 inches (50.8 cm) long.

2. Measure and mark the center points on two of the 31-inch (78.7 cm) pieces of copper pipe. Drill through both pipes at this point. Repeat this process on the two remaining 31-inch (78.7 cm) copper pipes.

3. Run one 2-inch (5 cm) bolt through the drilled hole on one 31-inch (78.7 cm) pipe. Thread a hex nut on the bolt, and then run it through the second pipe. Screw one cap nut onto the end of the bolt.

4. Repeat step 3 with the remaining two 31-inch (78.7 cm) pipes.

5. Dry fit the copper corner pieces onto the 31-inch (78.7 cm) pipes, and then the 20-inch (50.8 cm) pipes into the corner pieces to make two rectangles. Adjust the parts as needed to ensure a good fit.

6. Following the manufacturer's instructions, use the contact cement to glue all the corner pieces and pipes together. Let dry.

7. Measure and cut five pieces of the woven jute, each 24 inches (61 cm) long. Fold the corners of each cut end into a point, and machine- or hand-stitch in place.

8. Wrap both pointed and sewn ends of one jute strap around the 20-inch (50.8 cm) copper pipes. Adjust the length of the strap so the jute on the top of the pipe frame is 18 inches (45.7 cm) long. Hand-stitch the strap in place. Repeat to attach the remaining four straps to the copper frame.

cutting copper pipe & tubing

You can cut copper pipe with a hacksaw, but a manual pipe and tube cutter ensures a square cut every time. At the heart of this tool's design is a cutting wheel adjusted with rollers. To operate it, first unwind the cutter and insert the pipe. Carefully screw the cutter back in place so its wheel sits on the pipe where it needs to be cut. (If the pipe isn't mounted square to the rollers, the blade may score a spiral path along the pipe instead of making a circular revolution.) Turn the tool around the pipe. Once you've made a proper score, the blade is less likely to roam; there is now an established path for it to follow. Tighten the cutter after each turn. Increasing the pressure causes the wheel to eventually cut though the pipe at a right angle. When the cut is finished, remove the burrs inside the pipe with a half-round metal file.

Make a Stand

Assemble this handy pipe storage rack in a jiffy with a minimum amount of muss and fuss. Add one (or two) to expand storage space in an existing closet or to organize textiles at a sewing station. Hooked over the pipe, trouser hangers can hold cloth, paper, or even business files should you be so moved.

You Will Need

2 lengths of threaded galvanized pipe*

Galvanized steel 90-degree elbow joint to fit pipe

2 galvanized steel floor flanges to fit pipe

4 to 8 screws, depending on the number of floor flange screw holes

*The lengths of the pipes will vary according to where and how you use the rack. You'll find the threaded pipe at home improvement stores in standard lengths such as 18, 24, and 30 inches (45.7, 61, and 76.2 cm).

1. Determine how far you'd like the rack to extend. This will determine the length of one galvanized steel pipe to purchase. Buy the second pipe according to the height you desire your rack to be. (Home centers have a variety of threaded pipe lengths to choose from.)

2. Tightly screw one end of each length of galvanized steel pipe into the 90-degree elbow joint.

3. Thread one floor flange on the open end of each galvanized steel pipe, and firmly twist to secure.

4. Fasten the pipe rack to the wall and floor with screws.

Pipe Island

Configure this versatile kitchen worktable any way you choose. The dimensions of the tabletop you purchase will dictate the size of the island unit. We used an inexpensive pine tabletop measuring 20 x 40 inches (50.8 x 101.6 cm), but you could invest in a custom-sized hardwood butcher-block top for increased durability.

You Will Need

Pine board tabletop, 1 x 20 x 48 inches (2.5 x 50.8 x 121.9 cm)

Polyurethane finish (optional)

Cleaning solvent or label remover solvent

4 galvanized steel threaded pipes, 1 x 18 inches (2.5 x 45.7 cm)

4 galvanized steel threaded pipes, 1 x 12 inches (2.5 x 30.5 cm)

2 galvanized steel threaded pipes, 1 x 30 inches (2.5 x 76.2 cm)

Abrasive pad

Plumber's tape

4 galvanized steel T-connectors, 1-inch (2.5 cm) diameter

Pipe wrench

4 galvanized steel flanges, 1-inch (2.5 cm) diameter

Drill and drill bits

16 wood screws, ¾ inch (1.9 cm)

Screwdriver

Handsaw

Wood dowel, 1-inch (2.5 cm) diameter, 12 inches (30.5 cm) long

4 casters

Half-round file

2 galvanized door pulls, 4 ⅞ inches (12.4 cm)

Storage baskets (optional)

1. If desired, finish the pine board tabletop with the polyurethane before assembling the table.

2. Use the cleaning solvent to remove any labels and oily residue from the galvanized steel pipes, and then scour the pipes with the abrasive pad. Set them aside.

3. Wrap a short length of the plumber's tape on the threaded ends of the 30-inch (76.2 cm) pipes. Attach the center portion of each T-connector to each end of the pipes. Use the pipe wrench to tighten the connection. Check to see that the T-connectors lie flat on the floor without rocking. They must be parallel; adjust them if necessary.

4. Wrap the tape on the threaded ends of the 18-inch (45.7 cm) lengths of pipe. Attach one end of each pipe to one end of each T-connector, and tighten them with the pipe wrench. These pieces form the upper parts of the table legs.

5. Attach a flange to the other ends of the 18-inch (45.7 cm) pipes.

6. Lay the pine tabletop face down on a flat working surface. Set the assembled sections with the flanges on the underside of the tabletop. Center the sections on the top, and mark the points for the screws. Use the

drill and appropriate size bit to drill shallow pilot holes in the tabletop. Attach the flanges to the tabletop with the wood screws.

7. Use the handsaw to cut the dowel into four lengths, each 3 inches (7.6 cm) long. Select a bit comparable to the stem of your casters. Drill a hole centered on one end of each dowel length, deep enough to insert a caster. Insert a dowel into one end of each piece of 12-inch (30.5 cm) pipe. You may need to file the interior of the pipe with the half-round file to remove burrs. If you don't have a file, use coarse sandpaper to reduce the diameter of the dowel to fit inside the pipe. Set the dowels aside.

8. Wrap the plumber's tape on the other ends of the 12-inch (30.5 cm) pipes, and screw them into the remaining openings on the T-connectors. Tighten them with the pipe wrench. These pieces form the bottom parts of the table legs.

9. Ask someone to help you turn the table right side up. Then, have your helper lift one table end, while you insert a caster into a dowel, and slip it inside one of the pipe legs. Repeat with the other leg, and then with both legs on the other end of the table.

10. Attach the door pulls on the front side of the table, using the hardware packaged with the pulls. Place storage baskets across the base pipes, if you like.

Variation

If you want a stationary table, skip the steps for adding casters. Instead, fit rubber caps over the bottom ends of the 12-inch (30.5 cm) pipes.

Rolling Screen

Define your own private space, or section off a room with this three-panel rolling screen. Because it's on wheels, the screen can be relocated at a moment's notice. The pipe frame is a sturdy and durable structure that can be dressed up or down with any fabric panels you choose. You may have to special order these particular galvanized steel pipe connectors, but they'll make assembly a breeze.

You Will Need
For the screen frame:

Allen wrench

4 pin fittings*

6 galvanized steel pipes, each 6 feet (1.8 m) long, 1-inch (2.5 cm) diameter

4 eye fittings*

10 90-degree elbows*

4 galvanized steel pipes, each 1 foot (30.5 cm) long, 1-inch (2.5 cm) diameter

6 galvanized pipes, each 31 inches (80 cm) long, 1-inch (2.5 cm) diameter

2 three-socket tees*

2 side-outlet tees*

6 casters

*Kee Klamp® system fittings are used to make this screen. They differ from regular galvanized pipe fittings in that they are secured to the pipe with set screws. Fittings should be purchased to fit 1-inch (2.5 cm) diameter pipe.

For the screen panels:
Canvas or decorative fabric, 5 yards (4.6 m)

12 grommets, ½ inch (1.3 cm)

Grommet setter

Cording of your choice

1. Slide two of the pin fittings onto two of the 6-foot (1.8 m) lengths of galvanized pipe. Slide two of the eye fittings onto two of the 6-foot (1.8 m) pipe lengths. Set them aside.

2. Attach a 90-degree elbow at one end of each of the 1-foot-long (30.5 cm) galvanized pipes. Set them aside.

3. Assemble the screen frame as shown in the illustration on page 139. Use the pipes with the pin fittings to create the center panel. Use the pipes with eye fittings on the side panels. The three-socket tees are used on the bottom corners of the center panel. The side-outlet tees are used on one corner of both the side panels (place them opposite the pipes with the eye fittings).

4. Add the 1-foot-long (30.5 cm) galvanized pipes to the center panel's three-socket tees. Insert the casters in the elbow and side-outlet tees.

5. Cut the canvas or fabric to create three 28 x 75-inch (58 cm x 1.9 m) panels. Hem if desired.

6. Use the grommet setter to place grommets at the four corners of each panel.

7. At the top, bottom, and sides of each panel, secure the fabric to the screen with short lengths of cording (see detail, page 59).

> **What's an Allen Wrench?**
> An Allen wrench is a simple hand tool. It's a short, L-shaped, hexagonal bar used to fasten and unfasten screws and bolts with hexagonal sockets. Allen wrenches range in diameter from $\frac{1}{20}$ to $\frac{3}{8}$ inch (1.3 to 9.5 mm) and are often sold in sets on a ring. Other common names for Allen wrenches include *setscrew wrench*, *hex-key wrench, hexagon key, hex-L*, and *L-wrench*.

Pipe Pot Rack

Say good-bye to the frustration of disorganized pots and pans, and hello to this helpful and attractive hanging rack. From wok to colander, stock pot to steamer, it's always a relief to know exactly where your kitchen tools are stored.

You can modify this pot rack to suit your space. The lengths of galvanized steel pipe and number of connectors and flanges you need will depend on your design. The additional materials and tools you'll need to assemble and install the rack are similar to those listed under "You Will Need" for Make a Stand on page 54 and Pipe Island on page 57.

1. Locate the ceiling joists and the wall studs in the area where you want to hang the rack. For stability, you'll want to anchor the rack into structural supports.

2. Based on your anchor points, determine the rack's design. A simple square is fine. You also may want two levels of hanging bars, like those on the rack shown here. The higher bar is for pots and pans with long handles. The lower bar makes it easy to reach kitchen tools with shorter handles.

3. Purchase the galvanized steel pipes and connectors, and clean them (see step 2, page 57).

4. Use plumber's tape and a pipe wrench to connect the pipe pieces, according to your design.

5. Attach the flanges to the end pieces.

6. Screw the flanges into your ceiling and, if necessary, your wall, making sure the screws are long enough to reach into the joists and/or studs.

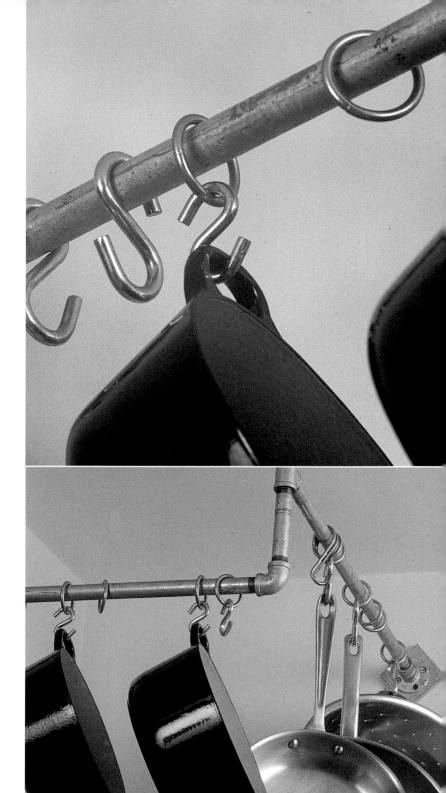

King-of-the-Grill Tray

With retro-styling all the rage, what better old-school accessory to reinvent than the TV tray? This contemporary version, however, merits more than a bland frozen dinner. Its sleek copper-pipe legs fold in and out for easy storage. The circular grill top in a contrasting metal is both good looking and sturdy, two timeless qualities for any outstanding design.

You Will Need

Pipe cutter

2 copper pipes, each 10 feet (3 m) long, ½-inch (1.3 cm) diameter

Steel wool

Polyurethane spray

Drill and drill bit

2 bolts, 2 inches (5 cm)

2 hex nuts to fit bolts

2 cap nuts to fit bolts

8 copper 90-degree elbow joints, ½ inch (1.3 cm)

Contact cement

8 large washers, wider than the distance between the grill crossbars

4 round-head plated machine screws, each ½ inch (1.3 cm)

4 gripper clips, each ⅜ to ⅝ inch (.95 to 1.6 cm)

Round barbecue grill top

8 small washers

4 nuts, ½ inch (1.3 cm)

1. Use the pipe cutter to cut four pieces of the copper pipe, each 24 inches (61 cm) long. Cut four more pieces of copper pipe, each 17 inches (43.2 cm) long.

2. Clean the copper pipe pieces with steel wool, and then spray them with the polyurethane to keep them shiny.

3. Drill a hole at the center of each 24-inch (61 cm) pipe.

4. Run one of the 2-inch (5 cm) bolts through one of the drilled holes, and then add a hex nut to the bolt. Feed the same bolt through a second piece of 24-inch-long (61 cm) pipe, and then screw a cap nut on the end of the bolt. Repeat this step with the remaining two 24-inch (61 cm) pieces of copper pipe.

5. Dry fit the copper elbow joints onto the 24-inch (61 cm) pipes. Dry fit the 17-inch-long (43.2 cm) pipes onto the elbow joints to make two complete rectangles. Adjust the positions of the pipes and fittings as needed. Use the contact cement to glue all the copper pieces together. Let dry.

6. Place one large washer onto a machine screw, and then feed the screw through the hole in the gripper clip. From under the barbecue grill top, hold the flat side of one gripper clip between and parallel to the first two full-length crossbars. While holding the clip in place, put a second large washer on the screw, then a small washer, and finally a nut. Screw the elements tightly in place. Repeat this step three more times, once for each matching edge of the grill top.

7. To secure the tray, slide the gripper clips onto the top copper pipes of the table base.

Shelf Solutions

Pipe is such a versatile, durable, inexpensive, and attractive building material, that we wonder why more people don't incorporate it into their home design. Install this multilayered shelving unit in the bathroom to store frequently used items or build it in the living room to create a personal library or picture display.

You Will Need

Allen wrench

9 rail supports*

3 galvanized steel pipes, each 4 feet (1.2 m) long, 1-inch (2.5 cm) diameter

8 single-socket tees*

2 galvanized steel pipes, each 6 feet (1.8 m) long, 1-inch (2.5 cm) diameter

6 extra-heavy flanges*

2 90-degree elbow joints*

2 galvanized steel pipes, each 1 foot (30.5 cm) long, 1-inch (2.5 cm) diameter

Assorted wood screws

Wood glue

Finish nails

3 pieces of quarter-round molding, each 3 feet (.9 m) long

3 lengths of 1 x 8 board, each 3 ½ feet (1.1 m) long (for the shelves)

Paint and paintbrush

Screwdriver

1 x 8 wood for the storage box**

*Kee Klamp® system fittings are used to make this shelf. They differ from regular galvanized steel pipe connectors in that they are secured to the pipe with set screws. Fittings should be purchased to fit 1-inch (2.5 cm) diameter pipe.

**Exact measurements for the storage box are not given. Assemble the shelf, and then measure the exact distance from flange to flange. Use this measurement to create a simple box form for the bottom shelf, or purchase a ready-made box.

1. Slip three rail supports on each of the 4-foot (1.2 m) lengths of galvanized pipe.

2. Slip four single-socket tees on each of the 6-foot (1.8 m) lengths of galvanized pipe.

3. Attach one extra-heavy flange at the bottom of each of the 6-foot (1.8 m) pipes.

4. Attach a 90-degree elbow joint at the top of each 6-foot (1.8 m) galvanized pipe.

5. Attach the 1-foot (30.5 cm) pipes and the flanges to the 90-degree elbow joint.

6. Level the single-socket tees on the long pipes. Attach the 4-foot (1.2 m) pipe lengths to the single-socket tees.

7. Secure the shelf unit to the wall and floor with the appropriate screws.

8. Use wood glue and finish nails to secure the quarter-round molding strips to the wood shelves. If you have a router, you can create a channel for glass or clear plastic sheeting strips as shown in the photo. Paint the wood shelves as desired.

9. Use wood screws to attach the shelves to the rail supports.

10. Attach one extra-heavy flange to each of the bottom rail supports. Measure the distance between the two flanges. Construct a simple box based on that measurement in much the same way as you construct the cube shelves on page 89.

11. Paint the storage box as desired, and then secure it between the flanges with screws.

Above: An array of taper candles are held upright by fittings from the plumbing and electrical aisles, such as a reducing coupling, a compression coupling, and a copper adapter.

Left and below: Votive and pillar candles burn brightly as they rest in holders from the plumbing, electrical, building materials, and lumber departments. Examples pictured include a crimped duct reducer/increaser, a set screw coupling, a knock out seal, and a galvanized cap.

brilliant candleholders

Create fashionable candleholders with home center supplies from every department. The choices are abundant. In these photographs, we grouped the holders by candle size to showcase the range of their abilities. Whether you wish to set a romantic table with tall thin tapers or illuminate your living area with an array of votives, stylish hardware holders can satisfy your every need.

Pop Art

Let the prominent profile of these fence-cap candleholders (left) add an architectural touch to your home. The caps, sold in both silver and black, look great right off the shelf, or you can connect two to create a more sculptural appearance. To make a double-stack holder, simply use an awl to drill a hole in the center of two caps. Make the hole the same diameter as your pop rivets, and then rivet the two caps together. Who knew such a chic style could be fashioned so easily?

Cutting Edge

This garden-edging candleholder (below) has natural charm. Its rough-hewn wood melds seamlessly into a rustic decor, or it can be a pleasing contrast to modern metal and glass surfaces. The staggered heights of its 3-inch (7.6 cm) round logs creates two levels for candles. The edging is flexible, so you can curve your new candleholder in any direction. Sand the wood if you wish, or leave it coarse and rugged. You even could paint or stain the logs to introduce a bit of color.

Lighting & Electrical Departments

While shopping in any home improvement center, you can brighten up your experience by walking down the lighting and electrical aisles. The shelves are lined with fixtures and fittings, plate, tapes, and receptacles that are sure to illuminate your creative desire—and you can relax knowing you don't have to be a master electrician to master hardware-inspired home decor projects!

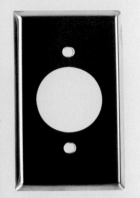

Conduit

Conduit is a protective pipe or tube through which electric wires or cables are run. Weighing one-third less than steel, rigid aluminum conduit makes an excellent choice for home decor projects. It can be easily cut, threaded, and bent without using special tools. Aluminum conduit is a low-maintenance material. It resists corrosion and will not leave discoloring streaks or stains. Electrical conduit is manufactured from other materials as well, such as steel and PVC, or *polyvinyl chloride*, a polymer used especially for electrical insulation, films, and pipes. And by no means does electrical conduit have to be rigid—there are flexible varieties (both metallic and non-metallic) with stylish ribbed surfaces that would add a modern feel to any room.

Conduit Fittings

Electricians use fittings to hold, join, or attach conduit. Specially designed couplings, connectors, and clamps take care of every situation. With their stocky industrial shapes and seductive metallic shimmer, fittings made of die-cast zinc are nearly irresistible. Whether you're drawn to the futuristic composition of a set-screw coupling or intrigued by the stellar shape of a locknut, conduit fittings have plenty of decorative appeal.

Wall Plates

In many home improvement centers, this vast electrical category requires its very own aisle. Wall plates cover everything from heavy-duty power receptacles to the switchplates you use everyday. Perhaps you haven't paid much attention to the various plate configurations in your own home, but give it a moment's thought and you'll realize that light switches, power outlets, phone jacks, and television cable all require different openings. (Combination and decorative plates fill the aisles even more!) These ready-made holes just beg to be filled with anything you can imagine, so the next time you have a picture to frame or an ikebana to arrange, why not head straight for the electrical department?

Lamp Parts

From clear to colored glass, smooth to rippled surfaces, bulbous globes to flat platters, the lighting department provides you with a fixture fitting for every home decorating idea. There are replacement parts and accessories galore for ceiling fan bulbs, chandeliers, and table lamps. Individual lamp parts also come in handy. Finials, harps, and threaded rods all have many alternate uses.

Electrical Tape

Electrical tape comes in a rainbow of colors and is a simple way to make a project vibrant. Usually ¾-inch (1.9 cm) wide, electrical tape is made from thin plastic. Most often used to cover bare wire after it has been stripped of insulation, electrical tape deftly conforms to curved surfaces.

Undeniably charming, charger plates are very practical as well. When setting a table, use them instead of place mats, one charger per guest. Chargers protect your linens by catching food spills and splatters. They also prevent heat and condensation from damaging wood surfaces. If you are handling hot plates of food, you can comfortably carry them on top of chargers. You also can chill chargers in the refrigerator to use with cold dishes such as fruit salad and gazpacho.

This wonderful charger is from the home improvement center. It's an inexpensive semi-flush shade for a ceiling light fixture. A shallow glass circle with a 13-inch (33 cm) diameter, the shade is wide enough to accommodate a regular dinner plate or soup bowl. This particular model has a white finish and a motif of tiny clear dots that can be dressed up or down to fit any occasion.

Ceiling to Table Charger

If you've dined in an elegant restaurant lately, you've probably noticed a large shallow dish, or *charger*, already on the table before you're seated. During the course of the evening, other plates and dishes are placed, or loaded, on top of it. The term charger stems from either the Anglo-Norman *chargeour* meaning "that which loads," or from the Old French *chargeoir* meaning "a utensil that is used to load."

Got-You-Covered Frame

Picture your family snapshots framed in electrical supplies. There are literally hundreds of options from which to choose. From this galvanized steel receptacle to socket plates and switch covers, the possibilities are endless. Each time you receive a new photo, take the framing challenge and survey your home improvement center looking for bright ideas.

You Will Need

Square surface cover for single receptacle, 4 inches (10.2 cm)

Clear acrylic sheet, 2 ¾ x 3 inches (6.9 x 7.6 cm)*

Drill and drill bits

Mat board, 2 ¾ x 3 inches (6.9 x 7.6 cm)

Nuts and bolts**

*Most home improvement centers will custom-cut your acrylic sheet to size.

**You'll need two 3-inch-long (7.6 cm) bolts to stand the frame. They need to fit the screw holes on two corners of the single-receptacle surface cover. Try out the bolts you've chosen. If your cover doesn't stand as you'd like, use longer bolts. You'll also need to purchase four small bolts and nuts to replace the screws on the cover. They should be at least ½ to ⅝ inch (1.3 to 1.6 cm) long.

1. Remove any screws that are attached to the single-receptacle surface cover.

2. Center the acrylic sheet on the back side of the single-receptacle surface cover. Mark the position of the cover's screw holes on the acrylic sheet. Drill the marked holes in the acrylic sheet.

3. Use the acrylic sheet as a guide to mark the position of the screw holes on the mat board. Drill the holes through the mat board, or simply pierce them with an awl.

4. Sandwich your photo between the mat board and the acrylic sheet. Secure the photo to the frame with the small nuts and bolts.

5. Insert the long bolts into the bottom two corners of the frame to create the stand.

Decked-Out Jelly Jar Vases

Jelly jar porch lights have a classic silhouette and a nostalgic charm that suggest the carefree spirit of an earlier time. Inexpensive replacement glass for these classic fixtures is still sold in the lighting department of hardware stores.

These curvaceous fixtures make great vases for small flower arrangements. You can leave them plain or spice them up with patterns of vivid color cut from electrical tape. Electrical tape comes in a wide variety of cheerful tones, so you'll find just the right shades to complement your summer bouquets.

You Will Need

3 glass jelly jars, each 7 inches (17.8 cm), 4 ½-inch (11.4 cm) diameter

Glass cleaner

Paper towels

Purple, orange, and yellow electrical tape, one roll of each

1. Remove all labels from the jelly jars, and clean their surface with the glass cleaner.

2. Use the purple electrical tape to create a horizontal band of color around the center of one jelly jar. (Electrical tape is very flexible and will conform to curved surfaces with a little coaxing.) Smooth out any air bubbles or wrinkles in the tape as you adhere it to the glass.

3. Cut a small rectangle of yellow electrical tape, and then cut the rectangle from corner to corner to form two triangles. Adhere these two rectangles to the purple band applied in step 2. Repeat this step until you've adhered enough yellow triangles to encircle the jelly jar.

4. Cut four bands of the yellow electrical tape, each measuring one-quarter of the distance around the central part of the jar.

5. Apply one horizontal band along the bottom edge of the central part of the jar. Starting at its upper right corner, apply the next horizontal band along the top edge of the central part of the jar. Repeat this sequence with the remaining two yellow bands. (Stretch the corners and ends of the tape as needed to make the bands meet.)

6. Cut eight small leaf shapes out of the orange electrical tape. At the end of each yellow band applied in step 6, adhere one leaf at a angle.

7. For the third jelly jar, use the orange electrical tape to make evenly-spaced vertical stripes around the center of a second jelly jar. Cut small circles out of the purple electrical tape, and apply one to the center of each orange stripe.

Medallion Mirror Magic

It's no secret that you can hang a mirror and instantly make any room feel larger. Without the weight of wood or the expense, a ceiling medallion can be transformed into a decorative mirror frame. Paint or stain the plastic to your liking, screw on a hanging wire, attach a mirror, and voilà—home center magic.

You Will Need

Ceiling medallion of your choice (ours has a 16-inch [40.6 cm] diameter with a 4-inch [10.2 cm] hole diameter)

White primer, if medallion is not primed for painting

Paintbrush

Spray paint, copper

Latex interior paint, light blue

Soft cloth

Latex interior paint, white

Fine-grit sandpaper

Clear acrylic spray varnish

Epoxy

Mirror to cover center hole (ours is round with an 8-inch [20.3 cm] diameter)

2 utility hangers

Picture wire

Wire cutters

1. If needed, paint the ceiling medallion with the white primer, and let dry.

2. Following the manufacturer's instructions, apply two to three thin even coats of the copper paint to the ceiling medallion. Let the paint dry completely between coats.

3. Use a paintbrush to apply a coat of the light blue latex interior paint on top of the copper-colored medallion. While the paint is wet, use a clean soft cloth and randomly rub a small amount of white paint into the light blue paint. This creates a mottled tone on the surface of the medallion. Let the paint dry.

4. Gently sand the raised ridges of the ceiling medallion's relief design to expose portions of the underlying copper paint. Wipe any debris off the painted medallion after sanding.

5. Following the manufacturer's instructions, seal the painted medallion with clear acrylic spray varnish. Let dry.

6. On the front side of the painted medallion, use the epoxy to adhere the mirror over the center hole. Adhere the utility hangers to the back side of the medallion, above the center hole and approximately 4 inches (10.2 cm) apart.

7. Cut a length of the picture wire 4 inches (10.2 cm) longer than the space between the utility hangers. Feed one end of the wire through one utility hanger, and tightly twist the end of the wire around itself to secure. Feed through and twist the second wire end.

What's a Ceiling Medallion?

A circular medallion is a traditional way to add architectural interest to an otherwise dull ceiling. They are attached around the base of a ceiling fan or a hanging light fixture, and then painted or stained to match the decor. Modern ceiling medallions are molded from a urethane plastic that is lightweight and won't deteriorate. They come with a hole cut in the middle that can be enlarged with a jigsaw as needed. Surrounding the central hole, the plastic is often fashioned into a design. From sloping and restrained concentric circles to elaborate botanical patterns of vines and leaves, there are many styles from which to choose.

Rusted Locknut Screen

You can produce the warm tones of a rusty patina on shiny new hardware with less effort and in less time than you might imagine. Soaking metal objects overnight in a hydrochloric acid and water solution does the job efficiently. Use the plans provided to create your hardware screen, altering the width and height as you wish to fit your room. Once you have the rebar screen fabricated for you by a local welder, all that's left for you to do is enjoy stringing the links together.

You Will Need

Screen plan (see page 140)

6 steel rods (rebar), each ½ inch (1.3 cm) x 10 feet (3 m) long

4 metal hinges, each ¾ x 3 inches (1.9 x 7.6 cm)

Hydrochloric acid (also sold as muriatic acid, a swimming pool supply)

Bucket

Assorted screen hardware, such as: 1 ½- and 3-inch (3.8 and 7.6 cm) S hooks; and 1-, 1 ¼-, 1 ½-, and 2-inch (2.5, 3.2, 3.8, and 5 cm) conduit locknuts

Clear spray varnish (optional)

1. Take the plan to several welding shops to get the best estimate for fabricating the rebar screen. Have the screen built to your specifications, using the rebar and hinges.

2. While the screen is being built, you can prepare the hardware. Following the manufacturer's instructions for safely handling the hydrochloric acid, make a solution in the bucket that is three parts water to one part hydrochloric acid. Place all the screen hardware, the S hooks and locknuts, into the bucket. Let the hardware sit in the solution overnight.

3. Remove the hardware, but don't dry off the solution. Let the hardware *oxidize*, or sit in the air.

4. Randomly string together lengths of hardware into chains. Hang the hardware chains from the top crossbars of the rebar screen.

What's a Conduit Locknut?

A very narrow ring of zinc-plated steel with six flat protrusions, locknuts are used to secure conduit or tube fittings to an electrical box. They're manufactured in many sizes ranging from ½ to 2 inches (1.3 to 5 cm) in diameter. You can find conduit locknuts in the electrical department of your homeimprovement center.

What's Rebar?

The term rebar is short for *reinforcing bar*, a type of steel rod used in concrete construction. The ridges rolled into the bar as it's milled later anchor it mechanically into the concrete. Rebar is commonly ⅜, ½, or ⅝ inch (.95, 1.3, or 1.6 cm) in diameter. The overall diameter is about 1/16 inch (1.6 mm) larger than the *nominal* (or stated) size, because of ribs and deformations that slightly project. Grade 40 rebar, the softest type, is often found in homes and landscaping; grade 50 and grade 60 rebar are made from harder and stronger steel. Rebar is usually sold in 20-foot (6.1 m) lengths, but shorter lengths are available or can be cut at your home improvement center. To cut rebar yourself, you can use a hacksaw (see 10 Things You Should Know About Using a Hacksaw on page 133), a metal-cutting blade in a circular saw, rebar cutters, bolt cutters, or a saber saw with metal-cutting blades. Grade 40 rebar is easy to cut with a saw, but grades 50 and 60 are much more difficult.

Heavy Holders

Just a hint of hardware can energize a table setting. One small metallic touch that is both practical and adorable is the diminutive beam clamp. Made of malleable iron with an electroplated finish, these little gems can be found in the electrical department of any home improvement store.

Only 1 inch (2.5 cm) tall, a beam clamp's size belies its substantial weight. Super-sturdy and threaded with an adjustable, slightly angled bolt, a beam clamp makes a unique stand for place cards or menus on the dining table, recipe cards in the kitchen, or even photos at work. They also can handle deeper objects such as a stack of business cards or sticky notes.

the new napkin rings

Cloth napkins were once placed in personalized rings so family members could identify and reuse their linens at each meal. Today, napkin rings generally serve a more decorative purpose: they keep napkins in a certain form or design, and they beautify a table setting.

When choosing these accessories to grace your table, there are no formal guidelines to follow. The most important concern is to select materials that appeal to your unique sense of design.

It may be surprising that many options can be found at your home improvement center. From a simple metal ring to a black and orange plastic mini-clamp, we were pleased to discover new ideas for napkin rings on almost every aisle.

Lumber Department

The lumber department at your local home improvement center is a visually impressive area. Towering above you, sheets of plywood and lengths of timber are stacked on enormous scaffolding. Most customers procure their merchandise with the help of an employee with a forklift. If you find this spectacle overwhelming, here's a quick lesson in the fundamentals of wood.

Wood & Lumber

Softwoods are derived from conifers, mostly needle-leaved trees, such as pines, spruces, and firs. Hardwoods come from leaf-bearing trees, such as oak and maple.

Generally speaking, the term *lumber* refers to all sawed wood with a thickness equal to or exceeding 2 inches (5 cm). The thickness of a *board* equals or is less than 2 inches (5 cm). Timber is wood sawed into pieces larger than 5 x 5 inches (12.7 x 12.7 cm).

When wood is *dressed*, or sawed, sanded, and dried, it loses some wood from its original cut size. This makes the commonly used names, such as 2 x 4 and 1 x 4 (inches), inaccurate. Keep this discrepancy in mind when you shop for wood. (This distinction does not apply to manufactured wood products, such as plywood.)

Lumber is graded by the amount of defects, such as knotholes, it contains. *Clear* or *select* pieces have no or few defects, while *common* boards have varying flaws.

When selecting the right piece of wood, follow these helpful buying hints. First, check to see that the board is straight rather than warped. Note the location of any knots, and determine whether they will interfere with your project. (In many circumstances, you can buy common wood for less money, and work around knots and defects.) Broken lines running down a board's length may signify pitch or sap pockets that will eventually cause warping. Choose dried wood if possible; it can be nailed in place right away.

Wood Veneer

Veneer is an extremely thin surface layer of finely-grained wood, usually 1/40- or 1/28-inch (.6 or .9 mm) thick. Home centers sell wood veneer in strips similar to narrow rolled ribbon or in wide flat sheets. Many different wood grains are available.

Manufactured Wood Products

Manufactured wood products are made from wood that has been cut, chipped, shaved, or ground into particles of various shapes and sizes. These pieces are compressed under heat with synthetic resins and binders. There are many types of manufactured wood products, such as plywood, oriented-strand board (OSB), particleboard, hardboard, perforated hardboard (pegboard), medium density fiberboard (MDF), and fiberboard. Consult home center pamphlets or the Internet to learn more about the unique properties of these composite boards.

Millworked Lumber & Accessories

Some decorative wood pieces are so common and practical that home centers sell them precut and ready to use. These include molding, dowel rods, brackets, shelves, rosettes, appliques, and other carved wood specialties.

Sawhorse Table

If you're in need of a desk, computer workstation, or hobby or potting table, then look no farther than the lumber department of your home improvement center. Carpenters and other craftsmen have long known that you can make an on-the-spot table by attaching a sturdy surface on top of a set of sawhorses. Often relegated to the basement, workshop, or garage, these rugged, reliable supports can take the place of conventional table legs. We've even spotted some sawhorses underneath costly slabs of glass and granite.

There are many benefits of a sawhorse table. The first is strength. Commercial sawhorses can support up to 1,000 pounds (454 kg), easily enough muscle for a computer and all its valuable peripherals. Next is portability. Sawhorses are engineered to fold up for transporting, storage, and hanging. Some even have handles. This mobility could make a sawhorse table the ideal temporary home office or additional workstation. Last, but by no means least, is storage. Most sawhorses have a bottom shelf meant to hold tools. You can adapt this space with ease to make it hard-drive and file-folder friendly.

Wooden sawhorses, once the norm, are now rather difficult to find. Most home improvement centers carry sawhorses made from different materials such as heavy-duty plastic or galvanized steel. These contemporary versions look fabulous straight off the shelf, or you can customize them with paint to fit any color decor. We gave our sawhorses several coats of matte spray paint in a dark shade of indigo to contrast with the chrome office accessories. The final result has a sharp, clean, and very professional appearance.

Lattice
Bulletin Board

If you want to display interesting post-cards or keep tabs on important papers but find ordinary cork bulletin boards a bit dreary, this custom-colored lattice panel may be the answer. Simply use clothespins and clip your mail or other documents to its wooden slats for safe-keeping. (No more unpleasant pushpin holes!) Use unfinished wooden clothes-pins as shown, paint them if you wish, or use brightly colored plastic clips.

You Will Need
Handsaw

Pine lattice panel, 2 x 8 feet (.6 x 2.4 m)

Hammer or pliers

Sandpaper or electric palm sander

Spray paint, matte blue

Clothespins

1. Use the handsaw to cut the lattice panel to the size you desire.

2. Determine which side of the panel to use as the front of the bulletin board. Hammer down any staples that protrude from the surface of the lattice, or remove them with pliers.

3. Sand the cut edges of the lattice panel with the sandpaper or the electric palm sander. Since most lattice is made from low-grade wood, you also may want to sand the surfaces of the slats on the front side of the board.

4. Working outdoors or in a well-ventilated area, carefully apply thin even coats of spray paint to both sides of the lattice panel. Also paint its edges. For best results, work gradually and let the paint dry thoroughly between coats.

What's Lattice?
Lattice is a group of thin boards assembled in a crisscross fashion into panels of various sizes. Dividers, trellises, entryways, and deck screens are often created from lattice. An inexpensive and versatile material, lattice is used to disguise unpleasant sights, such as trash bins and air conditioning units, to provide privacy, and to act as a barrier.

measure for measure

The old adage "measure twice, cut once" can never be overstated. Accurate measuring pays off for both large and small home improvements. Here are two tips to increase the precision of your measurements and speed your work.

When drawing a line with a straightedge or a square, firmly place the pencil on the mark first, and then guide the ruler to meet it. If you position the ruler on the mark first, then you'll have to estimate how much to compensate for the pencil thickness. With a dull pencil point, this can result in a difference of as much as ⅛ inch (3 mm).

You may not know it, but "trusty" tape measures can give you wrong readings. The most common reason for inaccuracy is a bent hook at the end. To remedy this, you can do one of two things: slightly adjust the hook with pliers; or do what professional carpenters do and "burn an inch"—begin your measurement at the 1-inch (2.5 cm) mark instead of the hook.

Storage box*

Masking tape

Paint and paintbrush

Casters (optional)

Drill with screwdriver bit

Screws

Metal shelf and brackets

Handrail

Saw

2 to 6 handrail brackets

Large S hooks

Wooden hangers

*If you can't find a box, use an easily assembled drawer unit.

1. Measure the width of the box or drawer unit. Measure and mark this width on your wall. Mask one or both edges with masking tape.

2. Paint the exposed wall area; then paint the box or drawer unit to match the wall color.

3. If desired, attach casters to the bottom corners of the storage box.

4. Measure the height of the storage box (with casters, if using). Install a single metal shelf on the wall, accommodating the storage box underneath.

5. Measure and mark the handrail equal to the width of the painted area. Use the saw to cut the rails to that length.

6. At heights convenient to you, install the handrail brackets and handrails to the wall above the metal shelf, making sure they are level.

7. Hang the large S hooks and wooden hangers from the handrails to hold hats, jackets, or other odds and ends.

Mock Closet

So, you don't have a coat closet in your foyer? You don't have a foyer? Do you need extra storage space but don't want to build a closet? Assemble this stylish mock closet with a little ingenuity and a few items from the home improvement center. Using a bold color ties together the different units into a flattering composition.

Barnyard Bed

After a full day of riding the range, why not corral your darling into this playful pen? With the gate closed for the night, your child (and all of his animal kingdom) can peacefully drift off to dreamland feeling safe and secure until the cock crows at daybreak.

For easier assembly, create this fantasy bed from commercial fencing units. If you're an accomplished carpenter, however, you can design and construct the bed frame on your own, using this example for inspiration. Either way you choose, be sure to finish off the wood with a soft wash of color, and paint all of the hardware and oversized hinges in a bright contrasting tone.

The Contemporary Cube

Modular open storage units are practical, attractive, and quite easy to construct. Based on your needs, you can use simple wooden boxes to show off a single design accent or organize an entire music collection. Whether customized with paint or left unfinished, wall-mounted on cleats or made mobile with casters, the contemporary cube is a versatile home center project.

You Will Need

2 wood pieces for the cube's sides, each ½-inch (1.3 cm) thick

2 wood pieces for the cube's top and bottom, each ½-inch (1.3 cm) thick

Plywood piece for the cube's back (if using a back), ¼-inch (6 mm) thick

Wood glue

Hammer

Finishing nails

Wire nails or brads, ⅝ inch (1.6 cm)

Sandpaper

Paint, stain, or varnish (optional)

Small wood pieces, 1 x 2 (for wall-mounted cubes)

4 plate or ball casters (for rolling cubes)

1. Determine the wood measurements for the size cube you wish to construct, following these guidelines: the top and bottom wood pieces need to be 1 inch (2.5 cm) longer than the two side pieces; the back piece needs to be the same length as the top and bottom pieces. Cut the wood pieces to these measurements.

2. Assemble the cube by brushing a little wood glue onto the edges of the wood pieces, and then nailing the top and bottom to the sides. Check to make sure the cube is square. Apply a small amount of glue to the edges of the back piece (if using), and nail it in place, using the ⅝-inch (1.6 cm) wire nails or brads.

3. Smooth all the cut edges of the cube with sandpaper. Finish the unit as desired. For hanging cubes, cut a piece of 1 x 2 wood that is 2 inches (5 cm) shorter than the interior measurement at the top of the cube. For rolling cubes, attach one caster at each of the four bottom corners with screws.

What's a Caster?
Casters are the tires of the hardware world. Because they roll, casters are mounted on the base of both large and small objects to make them mobile. Depending on their function, casters come in many shapes and sizes. They are manufactured out of a wide variety of materials, such as rubber, plastic, and metal. Some are wheel-shaped, while others are spherical; some turn a full 360 degrees, while others roll only in a single plane. Stem casters have a vertical stalk that is inserted into a hollow leg, while plate and ball casters are topped with a flat surface with holes for screw mounting.

Suspended Shelves

If, like most people, you're on a perpetual quest to find enough surface area in your home to display your favorite objects, you'll certainly appreciate this inventive shelving design. The union of rich mahogany-stained wood with coarse rugged rope is surprisingly dignified. Hang it in any location by securing its rope arches over a plant hook or ceiling bracket.

You Will Need

2 oak shelf boards, each 8 x 24 inches (20.3 x 61 cm)

Drill

Large wood drill bit, $^{11}/_{16}$ inch (1.7 cm)

Sandpaper

Wood stain, dark mahogany

High-gloss polyurethane

2 foam paintbrushes

Rag

Thick rope, 16 feet (4.9 m) long, $^3/_4$-inch (1.9 cm) diameter

1. On both oak shelf boards, measure and mark four corner points. Each point should be 1 ½ inches (3.8 cm) in from both the ends and edges.

2. Use the drill and large drill bit to make a hole on the shelf boards at each point marked in step 1. Sand both boards, and then completely wipe off all dust and debris.

3. Following the manufacturer's instructions, stain both shelf boards to a dark mahogany finish, and let dry.

Apply two to three coats of the high-gloss polyurethane to seal and finish the stained boards. Let dry. Determine which piece of wood you wish to use as the upper shelf and which as the lower shelf. Cut the rope into two 8-foot-long (2.4 m) pieces.

4. Make a knot in the end of one piece of rope. Run the untied end of the same rope through one corner hole of the lower shelf from the bottom. Slide the lower shelf down the rope until it rests on the knot.

5. Measure 15 inches (38.1 cm) up the rope from the top surface of the lower shelf. Tie a knot in the rope, leaving approximately 9 inches (22.9 cm) from the top of the lower shelf to the top of the second knot.

6. Run the untied end of the rope up through the hole in upper shelf. Feed the same end of the rope down through the second hole on the same end of the upper shelf. Leave 25 inches (63.5 cm) of slack rope arching above the upper shelf. Tie a knot in the rope below the upper shelf.

7. Run the untied end of the rope through the last empty hole on the side of the shelf you've been constructing. Tie a knot under the lower shelf, leaving 9 inches (22.9 cm) between the top surface of the lower shelf and the top of the upper knot.

8. Repeat steps 4 through 7 to feed the second rope through, and tie off the other end of the shelf.

Low Ride Tables

Let these racy coffee tables propel your home's interior fashion into high gear. With a set of rolling casters underneath, these weighty tables are easy to steer. The oversized butcher-block style top can be constructed from chunky fence posts, a satisfactory substitute for milled lumber. If you have the equipment and know-how to mill lumber and create a perfect glued joint, your tables will look more like the models shown.

You Will Need

5 fence posts per table, each 4 x 4 inches (10.2 x 10.2 cm) and 6 feet (1.8 m) long*

2 x 4 lumber piece, 6 feet (1.8 m) long

Saw

Pipe clamps (optional, but handy)

Drill and drill bits

Wood screws, 3 ½ inches (8.9 cm)

4 casters

*Purchase the straightest fence posts you can find.

1. Measure and cut the fence posts into 36-inch (91.4 cm) lengths. You will have a total of 10 pieces.

2. Lay the fence post pieces on the floor, and push them together. They will roughly measure 36 inches (91.4 cm) both ways.

3. Measure and cut two pieces of 2 x 4 lumber, each 34 inches (86.4 cm) long. Set them aside.

4. If you have access to pipe clamps, use them to clamp the fence posts together. If you don't have pipe clamps, find a friend to help you with the next step.

5. Drill small holes on the broad side of the 2 x 4 lumber pieces near their ends. Center the drilled lumber pieces on the fence posts. Move the lumber pieces about 6 inches (15.2 cm) in from each end of the fence posts.

6. Screw the lumber onto one fence post. If someone is helping you, have them push the fence posts together as you place a screw into each fence post through the smaller lumber pieces.

7. Secure one caster at each corner of the table with screws. Turn over the table. (You may need a friend; it's heavy!)

Post Coatrack

This refined coatrack looks like a family heirloom, but it was created entirely from home center parts. To realize her vision, the designer wisely used a wide array of standard mill-worked lumber, such as the carved post, post cap, and shelf brackets. A deep mahogany stain enhances the wood's appearance, handrail brackets make distinctive coat hooks, and window locks used strictly for decoration add a harmony to the overall design.

You Will Need

Untreated carved porch post, 3 inches x 3 inches x 8 feet (7.6 cm x 7.6 cm x 2.4 m)

Drill with assorted bits to fit hardware

2 bolts, each ¼ x 3 inches (.6 x 7.6 cm)

Pair of sawhorses

Sandpaper, 120 and 220 grit

Post cap with screw

4 decorative corner shelf brackets with hardware

Lint-free rags

Protective gloves

Gel stain, mahogany

Steel wool

4 handrail brackets with hardware

4 window lock catches with hardware

1. Cut the porch post to a length of 6 feet (1.8 m). (You may have it cut at the home improvement center or cut it yourself with a handsaw or table saw.)

2. Use a ¼-inch (6 mm) bit to drill a 1-inch-deep (2.5 cm) hole, centered, into each end of the post. Screw a ¼ x 3-inch (.6 x 7.6 cm) bolt into each of the holes. Suspend the post between the sawhorses by hanging it from the exposed ends of the bolts.

3. Sand the post, post cap, and each shelf bracket until smooth. Wipe down each piece with a slightly damp, lint-free rag to remove sanding dust.

4. Apply a thin coat of the mahogany stain to the shelf brackets, post, and post cap by rubbing them with a stain-dampened rag. Smooth out any puddles or drips of stain that form on the surface of each piece as you work around it. When the stain is dry to the touch, lightly sand each piece with steel wool. Apply additional coats of stain until you achieve the darkness you desire. Do not sand the last coat.

5. Locate the metal plate on the back side of one shelf bracket. Measure the distance from the bottom edge of the bracket to each screw hole in the plate. Copy these measurements onto one side of the post, measuring from the bottom up. Use a drill bit that matches the shelf-bracket screws to drill holes through the marks on the side of the post. Twist the screws into the post.

6. Align the holes in the metal plate with the screws on the post, and slide the bracket into place. Repeat steps 5 and 6 to attach the remaining brackets to the bottom of the post.

7. Remove the screw from the top of the post, and twist the post cap into place. Set a clean rag under the post cap to protect it as it balances on the sawhorse.

8. Position a handrail bracket and window lock catch on one side of the top end of the post. (Place them at convenient heights for reaching and hanging clothing.) Use a ruler to check that each piece of hardware is centered on the post. Use a marker or sharp nail to mark the screw holes through the hardware onto the post.

9. Set the hardware aside, and drill pilot holes through each mark on the post. Reposition the hardware over the drilled holes, and screw in place. Follow the same steps for attaching the remaining hardware to the post to complete your coatrack.

A Passion for Pegboard

Get ready to get organized. Clear away those pesky piles of paper on your desk and control your clutter with this multipurpose, adaptable pegboard. Instead of banishing things into the black hole of yet another file cabinet, sort your mail, display current photos and drawings, hang your scissors and calendar, post invitations—and do it all with style. Like all pegboards, yours can be individually arranged and continually rearranged to meet your specific needs. This fresh concept is not only a space-saver, it will also help save your peace of mind.

You Will Need

Pegboard (a standard sheet is
2 x 4 feet [.6 x 1.2 m])

Handsaw

Paint and paintbrush (optional)

Furring strips

Spirit level

Drill and drill bits

15 wood screws

Before You Begin

It's important to remember that pegboard must be mounted so there's a little
bit of space behind the surface of the
board. This allows you to insert hooks,
pegs, and other devices through the
front openings, and then safely seat
them on the back side of the board so
they are fully weight-bearing.

1. Determine the measurements for the
pegboard. If desired, cut the board to
size with a handsaw. Paint the board the
color of your choice, or leave it in its
natural state.

2. Cut three furring strips, each to the horizontal length of the pegboard. (*Furring
strips* are thin pieces of wood approximately 1 inch [2.5 cm] thick.) Paint the
ends of the strips to match the pegboard if
you wish.

3. Find and mark the wall studs (see
page 21, Six Ways to Find a Stud). Use a
spirit level to draw horizontal guide lines
on the wall at the top and bottom edge
of the pegboard.

4. Use wood screws and a drill to mount
the furring strips to the wall along the guide
lines. Fasten the screws into the studs to
provide adequate support.

5. Use a drill to mount the pegboard to the
furring strips with wood screws. Arrange
your hooks and pegboard accessories in a
pleasing manner.

You may be familiar with standard metal
pegboard hooks. These heavy-duty steel
hangers have a wonderful industrial look and
can serve many purposes on your new
board. Home improvement centers carry
other commercial pegboard accessories,
such as empty jars and bins, that can be
put to very creative use. The things that
make our pegboard so exciting, however, are
its unconventional hanging devices and its
clever storage solutions.

The detail in the upper right corner shows
two ceiling register grilles recast as letter
sorters. Simply run a wood screw through a
pegboard hole at each of the register corners, and firmly fasten the screw into the
wall. (Add this accessory after the pegboard
is wall mounted.) Immediately to the right of
the registers you can see scissors being hung
on an S hook.

The detail in the lower right corner shows a
crisscross of elastic cording threaded
through the pegboard holes. You can use
one or two pieces of elastic, just make sure
to tie it off tightly on the back side of the
board. (If you wish to use this technique,
apply the cording before the board is mounted to the wall.) Fabric and craft supply stores
sell many interesting types of elastic cord,
such as the metallic silver variety shown.

tantalizing table bases

You can make a stunning table from home center supplies with little or no effort at all. Just place a piece of glass on a sturdy base, and call yourself a designer! This can be an incredibly satisfying feat for you, as well as a delight to the many admirers you'll attract.

Concrete Desires

Add a stroke of ruggedness to your home decor. These thickset tapered concrete blocks, better known as *deck foundations*, make terrific supports for a low glass-top table (right). The coarse finish of the concrete provides wonderful contrast to the smooth, polished glass. As shown, a single block shoulders either end of one long and narrow glass plane. However, this design would look equally handsome with flour blocks and a larger square of glass. Let your imagination inspire you to fashion the concrete coffee table of your dreams.

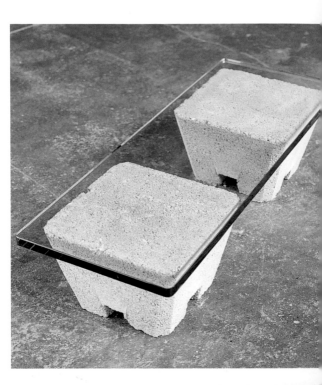

Ceramic Colonnade

You Will Need

2 tapered ceramic flower pots, each 10 inches (25.4 cm) tall, 12 ½-inch (31.8 cm) opening diameter, 8 ½-inch (21.6 cm) base diameter

Ceramic flower pot saucer, 11-inch (27.9 cm) diameter

Ceramic sealant spray

Heavy-duty ceramic-compatible adhesive

4 self-adhesive clear rubber bumpers

1. Spray all unglazed areas of the ceramic flowerpots and saucer with the ceramic sealant.

2. Using the heavy-duty ceramic-compatible adhesive, glue the large open ends of the two flower pots together. Let the adhesive completely dry.

3. Determine which end of the joined flower pots to use as the top of the table base. Glue the bottom of the ceramic saucer to the top of the table base, and let dry.

4. Evenly space the self-adhesive clear rubber bumpers on the top edge of the saucer to protect and grip the glass top. Place the glass on top of the table base. Display objects between the base of the saucer and the glass if you wish.

Just Can't Refuse!

Plastic goods look better than ever. Finally, color, texture, and shape are figuring in to the design of mass-marketed functional items. A perfectly simple vessel can hold great promise. It was love at first sight with this inexpensive but sturdy cherry-red wastebasket (right).

To create your own version of this unique table, shop for a wastebasket that appeals to you. (The walls don't have to be solid, but they must be strong.) While you're in the home improvement center, turn the wastebasket over to see how it looks upside down. Consider its contour and proportions. Once satisfied, take your new table base home.

If the base of your new table has a recessed area, you can fill it with all kinds of things before placing the glass on top. This example is packed with gray *paver sweep*, a sandy substance used for filling the gaps in garden paths and walkways. Pea gravel, marble chips, sea shells, marbles, nuts, washers—any of these would also make fantastic filler. You can even change the filler to suit the season or your mood (think of fall leaves, even peppermint candies). Top it off with a piece of beveled-edge glass—it can be any size, shape, or thickness you desire—and you've transformed a mundane object into a marvelous conversation piece.

Alluring Aluminum

How can you possibly resist something so stylish as the trendy end table pictured above? It has all the presence of designer furniture but is a stock item at your local home improvement center. Most often relegated to basements and closets, this table is more than qualified to assume its rightful place as a staple of hardware style. "What is it?" you may ask (and rightfully so!). The answer—a water heater stand.

To prevent explosion, plumbing codes require all gas water heaters to have their flame elements raised 18 inches (45.7 cm) from the floor. Traditionally, carpenters built wood stands, but now, safer, more durable steel products are available. Constructed of 18-gauge spangled galvanized sheet metal, this particular table is 18 inches (45.7 cm) high and has a 21-inch (53.3 cm) square top. Built to hold gas water heaters with a 30–50 gallon (25–41.6 British gallon) capacity, the table easily holds up to 650 pounds (295 kg). Because the metal is galvanized, you can put your drinking glasses or houseplants on it without fear of rust. It would also be great on a sunporch or deck, as it will withstand the elements like a true champion.

Building Materials Department

In most major home improvement centers, you'll find the building materials department snuggled up next to the lumber section. *Building materials* is a broad category, loosely describing all the non-wood elements needed for construction projects. When something needs to be set in cement or framed in metal, here you'll find what it takes to do the job. Building materials also keep you ventilated, insulated, drained, protected, and connected.

Metal Stock

Whether you buy it flat or angled, solid or slotted, common metal stock is one of the most attractive, durable, and versatile materials you can use right off the shelf to infuse your home with hardware style.

To provide the structural framework for many homes and buildings, carpenters rely on sturdy lengths of metal. Hidden behind walls stand various types of steel supports, such as angle iron, C-channel iron, and flat iron. The surface of these supports can be a solid or slotted sheet of aluminum, steel, or galvanized steel.

Metal Sheet Goods

Metal sheet goods are usually less than $^3/_{16}$ inch (5 mm) thick. They can be curved and cut easily without any special tools other than tin snips. Metals of this variety are sold in sheets

or on a roll. They often line walls next to heat-producing appliances such as stoves and fireplaces and also are used in various repair and hole-patching jobs.

Construction Connectors

Construction connectors are incredibly strong steel components designed to connect and strengthen roof, wall, floor, and foundation joints within the frame of a home and on decks

and fences. These cast metal fittings make jobs faster, easier, and less expensive for both weekend and professional builders. Construction connectors come in all shapes and sizes. To the average consumer, a single connector may look like a bizarre piece of bent, perforated, or serrated metal. This is just the characteristic that makes construction connectors eccentric, yet irresistible, decorating supplies.

Masonry Products

A mason is one who builds with stone or brick. Masonry products include everything a mason needs to do his job. Brick, blocks, stone, concrete, or any cement-like substances are all considered masonry products and all grouped with building materials.

Brick

All types of brick come from the same basic recipe: water mixed with clay and sand, and then baked. Brick's hardiness is proven by the fact that it is one of the few building materials that is routinely salvaged and reused. Although the most common brick size is 8 x 4 x 2 inches (20.3 x 10.2 x 5 cm), there are many other shapes (and colors, too) for whatever design application you may desire.

Concrete

To put it very simply, concrete is a mixture of cement, water, and an aggregate. Portland type 1 is the most common cement. It is sold at most hardware stores, home improvement centers, and building supply centers. Sand, gravel, and crushed stone are the most common aggregates. They are also easy to buy in bulk.

To create home decor accent pieces, such as the Cement Candle Tray on page 115, you can mix your own concrete or, for a slightly higher cost, purchase premixed concrete and just add water.

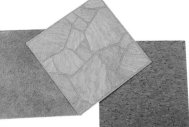

Vinyl Flooring

Vinyl tiles are the most common flooring materials used in commercial and residential buildings. Typically 12 inches (30.5 cm) square and $3/32$ to $1/8$ inch (2.3 to 3 mm) thick, they're available in many colors and styles. Vinyl tiles are either self-adhesive with peel-off backing papers or they're "dry-back" and must be laid in a bed of special adhesive, called *mastic*. Vinyl composition tile (VCT) contains recycled vinyl. It's more durable than plain vinyl and is frequently laid in industrial settings. Home centers also sell vinyl flooring in sheet form, cut to order off a roll.

Ceramic Tile

Ceramic tile has been around for centuries. It's a natural product made up of clay, minerals, and water. Thanks to modern technology, however, ceramic tile is now available in more colors, sizes, shapes, and textures than ever before. Many qualities make tile a superb building material, such as durability, versatility, easy care, fire-, water-, and scratch-resistance, and, of course, beauty.

Marble

Marble is a natural commodity. For this reason, no two pieces look exactly the same. Veining is inherent in all marble, and special sealants help protect it from staining.

Tempting Take-Out Box

Take your chopsticks, incense, or pencils "to go" in this clever container. To construct the box, cut and fold a single piece of aluminum roof flashing like a sheet of origami paper. Decorative rivets hold the sides together, and a wire handle completes the design. Reduce or enlarge the pattern to create multiple boxes with different dimensions if you wish.

You Will Need

Photocopied pattern, page 141

Aluminum flashing, 14 inches (35.6 cm) wide

Computer mousepad or craft foam mat

Embossing stylus or dry ballpoint pen

Metal ruler

Hammer

Nail or hole punch

2 rivets

Wire

1. Cut out the photocopied pattern, and trace it onto the aluminum flashing. Cut out the flashing in the pattern shape.

2. Place the aluminum flashing on top of the computer mousepad or foam mat. Place the photocopied pattern back on top of the flashing. Using the embossing stylus or dry ballpoint pen, firmly press along the dotted lines of the pattern. Use enough pressure to mark the flashing. Remove the paper pattern.

3. Place the metal ruler on top of the marked flashing. Use the embossing stylus or dry pen to reinforce the marks, and then fold the flashing up along the lines. Completely shape the box into position.

4. On both sides of the box where the aluminum flaps overlap, use the hammer and nail or punch to make a hole through all three pieces. Hammer a rivet into each hole to fasten the three flaps on both sides of the box.

5. Cut a 12-inch (30.5 cm) piece of wire, and fold it into a handle shape. Place the ends of the wire through the rivets, and turn them under to secure.

You Will Need

Marble threshold, 36 x 4 inches
(91.4 x 10.2 cm)

8 brass doorstops

Heavy-duty glue

1. Take the marble threshold to a ceramic tile cutter, or check with your home improvement center to see if they provide this service. Have the marble cut in half so you have two 18 x 4-inch (45.7 x 10.2 cm) pieces.

2. On the bottom side of both marble pieces, measure and mark a straight line 1 inch (2.5 cm) in from both ends. Measure and mark a point 1 inch (2.5 cm) in from each edge on the previously marked end lines.

3. Remove the screws from the ends of the doorstops.

4. Following the manufacturer's instructions, use the glue to adhere the door stops to the bottom side of the marble pieces, one at each marked point. Let the glue completely dry.

On the Threshold

Doorstop separators make impeccable supports, upholding the ambience of hardware style. When it's time for tea, you can use them to elegantly display your best demitasse cups, saucers, and spoons on thin strips of cool white marble. These miniature shelves express your high style without saying a word.

Tile & Post Support Trivets

Whether you use them on countertops or table tops, these swanky little trivets can really take the heat. Both in fashion and in function, clean white tiles poised atop aluminum feet are sturdy enough to stand the test of time.

This simple project is easily adaptable to suit your personal style. If you prefer slate or marble to ceramic tiles, go right ahead and make the switch. Perhaps you have some tile leftover from a recent renovation; or you picked one up as a vacation souvenir; or you like to hunt for antique tiles—here's an excellent opportunity to give any of these materials a new life. You also can paint the post supports any color you wish to enhance the final look.

You Will Need

Cast aluminum post standoffs
(post supports), 1 per trivet

Tiles

Paint (optional)

Epoxy or cyanoacrylate glue

1. Purchase the post supports from the home improvement center.

2. Select tiles for this project that are slightly larger than the post support.

3. Paint the post supports if desired.

4. Adhere the tiles to the supports with the epoxy or cyanoacrylate glue. Let the glue dry overnight before using the trivet.

> **What's a Post Standoff?**
> A post standoff or post support is type of construction connector (see page 100) used in fencing or decking projects. They're made from galvanized steel and generally sold in two sizes: 4 x 4 inches (10.2 x 10.2 cm) and 6 x 6 inches (15.2 x 15.2 cm).

Tasteful Trash Basket

To properly ventilate a structure, builders use many types of ducts and fittings. The home-center aisles on which these products are stored are a veritable wonderland of decorating supplies. Elbows, shanty caps, flexible ducts, hoods, and boots have an innate sculptural presence impeccably suited for modern home design.

This galvanized aluminum elbow is a twisting cylinder composed of four rotating parts. At the top of the elbow is a crimped ring of angled parallel grooves. This patterned rim adds a handsome texture, as do the elbow's pronounced raised seams and rivets.

To form a solid basket base, simply insert a round crimped plug at the bottom of the elbow. Align all four parts in a vertical formation as shown, or twist them at different angles for a touch of whimsy. Home centers sell many sizes of elbows and their appropriate plugs. The selection is so vast and the assembly so easy, you also could create an attractive set of elbow-inspired kitchen canisters, pencils holders, or bathroom storage accessories.

Good News Grid

Any love note or message left on this gorgeous board will surely get the attention it deserves. Some tiles are almost too pretty to be tread upon. You can choose any of the designer varieties from the home improvement center as long as they have a matte finish. Install additional tiles for a larger grid, or select smaller tiles to scale it down—the choice is yours!

You Will Need

4 ceramic tiles, 6 x 6 inches (15.2 x 15.2 cm) or the size of your choice; must have matte finish

Plywood, ¼ inch (6 mm) (optional)

Sawtooth or flat picture hanger (optional)

Epoxy glue

Ceramic edge tile

Ceramic tile mastic

Chalk

1. If you wish to create a portable grid, first position the four tiles, and then measure their dimensions. Next, cut a piece of the ¼-inch (6 mm) plywood to this measurement. Finally, attach the sawtooth or flat picture hanger to the back side of the plywood.

2. Whether you are constructing a permanent or a temporary grid, use the epoxy to glue the edge tile to one of the bottom tiles. The edge tile becomes the shelf for the chalk.

3. Following the manufacturer's suggested application procedures, affix the tiles directly to the wall or to the plywood backing with the ceramic tile mastic. Let dry.

Upscale Uplight

Uplights are thrifty can fixtures that can be used with great effect. Simply set them behind a plant or on a side table, plug them in, and watch them throw a dramatic pool of light. To further focus the illumination, create a shadow pattern, and enrich the uplight's overall appearance, wrap it with an ornamental radiator grille.

You Will Need

Flexible punched brass radiator grille, 24 x 36 inches (61 x 91.4 cm)

2 small spring clamps

Thin brass wire

Wire cutter

Metal uplight can

1. Roll the 24-inch (61 cm) end of the brass radiator grille to form two layers of metal. Once both 24-inch (61 cm) ends meet and form a solid seam, clamp them in place.

2. Cut 48 inches (1.2 m) of the thin brass wire. You'll use the wire as you would a shoelace to join both sides of the rolled brass radiator grille. Starting from inside the rolled grille at one edge, thread one end of the wire through a punched design on one side of the seam. Thread the opposite end of the wire through a punched design on the opposite side of the seam. Pull the ends of the wire equally to center it inside the rolled grille. Thread the ends of the wire back inside the roll on the opposite side, and then outside the roll to secure the seam.

3. Lace the wire ends down the edge of the rolled grille, crisscrossing the seam, until you reach the middle of the roll. At this point, twist the two wire ends together on the inside of the roll.

4. Repeat steps 2 and 3, starting from the opposite end of the rolled grille. When the ends meet, twist the wires together and cut off any excess.

5. Place the completed shade over the uplight can. The light's electrical cord can exit the back of the shade through one of the punched designs. Determine where you'd like this to happen, and then clip the bottom end of the grille at this point with the wire cutters. Push the cord through the clipped slit until it rests inside a punched hole.

Tile Floor Mat

Have you ever thought about decorating the floors in your home? Beyond traditional rugs and runners, there are countless options just waiting for you to consider. One way to create a bold composition of color for your floor is this cheerful floor mat made from vinyl composition tiles. You have a lot of space to work with underfoot, so let your imagination run wild.

You Will Need
Vinyl composition tiles, each 12 x 12 inches (30.5 x 30.5 cm), 1 white, 2 black, 3 teal

Metal ruler

Sharp utility knife

Black spray paint

Luan board, 2 x 3 feet (.6 x .9 m)

Heavy-duty construction-grade adhesive

Putty knife

1. Mark the two black vinyl composition tiles in half. Place the metal ruler on the center line of one tile. Score it several times by running the utility knife down the length of the metal ruler. This will cause the tile to split. Cut both tiles in half.

2. Cut one teal vinyl composition tile in half following the method described in step 1.

3. Following the manufacturer's instructions, spray paint the edges and the back side of the luan board. Let dry.

4. Lay out the vinyl composition tile design on the unpainted side of the board. Adhere one tile piece at a time by spreading the heavy-duty construction-grade adhesive on the back side of the tile with a putty knife, placing the tile on the board, and firmly pressing it in place. Let the floor mat dry a full 24 hours before using.

10 glue clues

1. Identify what type of glue you need for the job.

2. Read the label carefully.

3. Clean and dry the surfaces to be bonded.

4. Know the working time and drying time of your adhesive.

5. Apply adhesives in a well-ventilated area.

6. Test-bond the materials with the adhesive, if possible.

7. Use an even coat of adhesive.

8. Avoid contact with the skin or eyes.

9. Remove excess adhesive from surfaces as quickly as possible.

10. Keep all containers firmly closed so the adhesive won't dry out.

Popular Adhesives

Contact Cement
Contact cement provides a secure adhesion on a variety of surfaces. Apply it to both surfaces being joined, allow it to dry, and then bring the two glued surfaces together.

Cyanoacrylate
This type of adhesive dries in seconds and bonds a wide variety of surfaces, including both porous and non-porous materials. Most jobs require only a small amount of this super-strong glue.

Epoxy
Very strong and durable, epoxies consist of a catalyst and a hardener, which must be mixed in equal portions to form an adhesive. Epoxies take many forms, such as liquid, putty, and paste.

Hot Glue
Hot glue is easy to use, bonds a wide variety of materials, and dries quickly. Different types of hot glue melt at different temperatures and range in strength. A faster application and bonding of hot glue produces smoother results.

Polyurethane
A premixed liquid adhesive similar to epoxy, polyurethane glue is fairly new on the market. It is excellent for interior and exterior applications and can be used with a wide variety of materials as long as one of them is porous.

White Glue (Polyvinyl acetate)
White craft glue is the most common fixative. It's very effective for bonding light materials, simple to apply, and quickly dries clear.

Yellow Carpenter's Glue (Aliphatic Resin)
Used by woodworkers for decades, this glue frequently has a thick, rather creamy consistency. Aliphatic resin can also be used on other porous surfaces, such as paper and cloth.

You Will Need

2 cored bricks (for long-handle storage) or 1 cored and 1 paver brick (for short-handle storage)

Scrub brush or rag

White enamel paint, matte finish

Paintbrush, 1 inch (2.5 cm) wide

Small paintbrush

Clear spray varnish, satin finish

1. Carefully select attractive bricks from the home improvement center. Use an old scrub brush or rag to remove dust and debris from all surfaces of both bricks. (Remember to clean inside the holes.) You can break off irregularities that extend past the edges of the brick or leave them intact for added interest.

2. Use the 1-inch-wide (2.5 cm) brush and the white enamel to paint all surfaces and inside the holes of both bricks. Use the small paintbrush as needed to reach into cavities. Apply a thin, even first layer of paint, and let it dry. Add more coats of paint until you achieve the desired coverage and opacity.

3. Following the manufacturer's instructions, spray the clear varnish on the bricks. Apply at least two coats to seal, protect, and enhance the painted bricks.

Brick Brush Holder

Here's a clever storage solution for bathroom countertops that is not only practical but also simple to make, inexpensive, and, most of all, attractive. These stacked painted bricks can hold toothbrushes, make-up brushes, or anything with a long, narrow handle. You can adapt this style by painting your bricks to match your bathroom, or by using contrasting colors of unfinished brick, or bricks with different profiles and textures.

Are All Bricks Created Equal?

The five most common brick types are *building brick*, *face brick*, *fire brick*, *pavers*, and *antique* or *tumbled brick*. Most of these category names refer to the brick's function. Building bricks are used for construction. They are cored, meaning they have interior holes to reduce material and thereby weight. Face bricks are the solid ones visible on the outside of a structure and come in various colors, sizes, and shapes. You will find heat-resistant bricks lining fireplaces and other high-temperature areas. Pavers are installed underfoot for sidewalks, patios, and edging. Antique or tumbled brick is either recycled material or bricks manufactured to look timeworn.

Cement Candle Tray

Warm and inviting, a candle's glow can instantly put you at ease. Whether your preference is for tealights or pillars, tapers or colonnades, candles are a low-key and stylish way to illuminate your home. Who would have thought that the home improvement center would have everything you need to create this enchanting tray? A ready-to-use cement mix makes the work easier than ever before. Use scrap lumber to build the tray mold in any size or shape you desire.

You Will Need

Scrap lumber

Drywall screws

Drill and drill bits

Cooking oil

Pet food cans or tea lights

Ready-to-use Portland cement and sand mix

Bucket

Rubber gloves

Trowel or cardboard

1. Determine the size and shape you wish to make the candleholder. Cut three boards for the bottom and long sides of the mold.

2. Drill two or more holes along the length of two of the long boards, each approximately ⅜ inch (9.5 mm) from the edge. Use drywall screws to attach the long boards to the sides of the bottom board.

3. Use any size boards to cover the open ends of the mold. Measure the ends, and cut the pieces to fit if desired. Attach the end boards to the side boards and the bottom boards of the mold with drywall screws.

4. Rub cooking oil on the inside surfaces of the mold. Rub cooking oil on the outside surfaces of the pet-food cans or tealights. Place the cans or tealights open-side-down in the box. Arrange their positions as desired.

5. Prepare the cement mix following the manufacturer's instructions. Put on a pair of rubber gloves, and then fill the mold with the prepared cement. Carefully and thoroughly pack the cement around the cans or tealights.

6. Pick up the filled mold and tap it on the ground to remove any air bubbles. Smooth the exposed surface of the cement with a trowel or cardboard.

7. Allow the cement to set up overnight, and then unscrew the mold. Reuse the mold as many times as you wish.

Picture-Perfect Ledge

Create a primary focal point for any room by arranging framed photos on horizontal picture ledges. Multiple artworks can be displayed on these shallow shelves without additional nails and hangers. Not only will you reduce the number of holes in your walls, you'll also have the freedom to rearrange your pictures and add new ones in an instant. Best of all, they'll always be level.

This ledge is simply a stock piece of angle iron. Rather than providing structural support inside the walls, the angle iron now makes a strong decorative statement. Since the iron is *galvanized*, or coated with rust-resistant zinc, its color will remain vibrant and stable.

You Will Need
Measuring tape
Spirit level (optional)
Drill with screwdriver drill bit
4 wood screws
Galvanized slotted angle iron, 1 ½ x 1 ½ x 60 inches (3.8 x 3.8 x 152.4 cm)
16 hex nuts, each ⁵⁄₁₆ inch (8 mm)
4 U bolts, each ⁵⁄₁₆ x 2 x 3 inches (.8 x 5 x 7.6 cm)
S hooks (optional)

1. Locate the studs on the wall where you will hang the picture ledge. Refer to page 21 for helpful hints on finding a stud. (You can use wall anchors for security if studs are not available in the position you desire.) Position the angle iron at the height of your choice, and adjust it until it's level. Use the drill and the wood screws to attach the angle iron to the wall.

2. Thread a hex nut onto each end of each U bolt, and screw it in completely.

3. Determine where you want your pictures to stand, and find the center of that location. Place a U bolt, open side down, through the closest slot in the angle iron. Screw a hex nut onto both ends of the positioned U bolt. Leave the bottom hex nut loose, and adjust the U bolt to the depth of the picture frame.

4. Tighten the bottom hex bolts. Repeat this process as many times as needed to install all desired artwork on the top side of the rail.

5. To hang artwork from the bottom side of the picture rail, you can either repeat steps 3 and 4 with the open side of the U bolt facing down, or place S hooks or other similar hangers into the slots.

> **What's the Difference Between Iron and Steel?**
> Iron is an *element*, a material that can't be reduced to a more basic substance by normal chemical means. Steel is an *alloy*, a mixture of two or more metals. Steel contains iron plus carbon and may even have traces of other matter, such as manganese, chromium, nickel, tungsten, or cobalt.

Light Industrial Candle Shades

These hardworking industrial tie plates have more romantic features once fashioned into a simple shade. On all four sides, candlelight filters through their many openings and is reflected in their lustrous metal finish, adding a sophisticated touch to any setting.

You Will Need*

4 nail-on tie plates

Masking tape

2 pairs of pliers

12 to 24 split-ring lock washers
(also known as lock washers), 7 mm

Empty jar lid

Votive or small pillar candle

*for one shade

1. Remove all labels from the nail-on tie plates.

2. Align the holes of the tie plates. (There is usually a slight variation in their positioning.) Use a small piece of masking tape to mark the top of each plate. Set the tie plates aside.

3. Use a pair of pliers to grasp one lock washer on one side of its split. Use the second pair of pliers to gently open the lock washer. (Move the ends from side to side, not open and closed like a lobster claw. Only open the washer as much as needed to insert the metal you're joining.) Before opening all the washers you'll need for the shade, check the fit of a single one as described in step 4.

4. Lay two tie plates atop each other, matching the taped ends. Slide the opened lock washer through a matching pair of holes in the tie plates. This general-ly calls for some minor adjustments before you successfully join the two plates. You may need to widen the opening of the lock washer to make it easier to slide the washer through the holes.

5. Determine how many lock washers you'll need to fasten the four sides of the shade. Complete one side of the shade at a time, matching the taped ends as you go along. You're simply linking the tie plates to one another.

6. To finish the shade, tighten the lock washers one at a time by grasping each side of the split with a pair of pliers, and gently returning them to a closed position.

7. Set a votive or other small pillar-type candle in a commercial holder or on a used jar lid and place it inside the tie-plate shade.

> **What's a Split Ring Lock Washer?**
> A washer is a flat disc, in this case metal (although they can also be plastic, rubber, and even leather) placed beneath the head of a nut or bolt to ease friction and distribute pressure. A split ring lock washer has one cut across the disc surface, causing a small but significant spring-like spiral. Once firmly in place this spiral shape creates enough pressure to keep nuts from loosening.

Home-Sweet-Home-Center Lamp

With its pipe base, nut-and-bolt feet, flashing shade, and chain trim, this lamp is the epitome of hardware style. The pipe and flange provides a solid base as well as an excellent visual contrast to the aluminum flashing's shine. Choose any variety of chain you desire to fashion the playful metal "fringe."

You Will Need

Galvanized steel pipe nipple, 1 x 12 inches (2.5 x 30.5 cm)

Galvanized steel floor flange, 1 inch (2.5 cm)

4 bolts, each ¾ inch (1.9 cm) long, ⅝-inch (1.6 cm) diameter

4 hex nuts, ⅝ inch (1.6 cm)

Lamp kit

Lampshade kit

Aluminum flashing

Contact cement

Hole punch

Wire cutters

Bead chain, 8 feet (2.4 m)

Small chain, 8 feet (2.4 m)

Pliers

Black double-fold bias tape, ½ inch (1.3 cm) wide

Hot-glue gun and hot glue

1. Screw one end of the galvanized steel pipe nipple into the galvanized steel floor flange.

2. Feed one ¾-inch-long (1.9 cm) bolt into each of the four holes on the top side of the floor flange. Screw one hex nut onto the end of each bolt to create the lamp's feet and to make room for the cord to exit.

3. Following the manufacturer's instructions, install the lamp kit into the top opening of the galvanized steel pipe nipple.

4. Use the template from the lampshade kit to draw the shape of the shade onto the aluminum flashing. Extend the bottom of the traced pattern by ¾ inch (1.9 cm). Cut the shade shape out of the flashing with scissors.

5. Following the manufacturer's instructions, use the contact cement to glue the aluminum flashing onto the shade. Let the flashing overhang the bottom edge of the shade by ¾ inch (1.9 cm). Let the glue dry.

6. Use the punch to create holes approximately ¾ inch (1.9 cm) apart around the bottom edge of the shade.

7. Use the wire cutters to cut the bead chain into 6 ½-inch (16.5 cm) lengths; then cut the small chain into 2 ¾-inch (7 cm) lengths.

8. Open one end of one small chain piece with wire cutters. Feed the open link through one punched hole, and then close the link with pliers. Repeat this step on every other hole around the base of the lampshade.

9. From the front side of the shade, feed one end of one ball chain piece through an empty hole at the base of the shade. Pull the ball chain from the inside of the shade, and then feed it back out through the next empty punched hole. Pull the ends of the ball chain back and forth as needed to make them even and to match the lengths of small chain. Dab a bit of contact cement on the inside of the shade to hold the bead chain in place. Repeat this step all the way around the base of the lampshade.

10. Use a hot-glue gun and hot glue to adhere the edge of a strip of black bias tape around the top of the lampshade. Fold the tape over to the inside of the shade, and secure it with hot glue at several points. Starting at the seam in the rear of the shade, use the hot-glue gun to adhere the bias tape over the punched holes around the bottom of the shade.

high-roller coasters

Drink coasters are sensible, yes, but they certainly don't have to look frumpy or old-fashioned. Here are six ways to create tiny works of art you'll be proud to display on your table and happy to use anytime.

A Touch of Vinyl

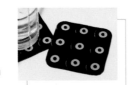

You Will Need
Molded black vinyl floor runner, raised circle design

Contact cement

Approximately 9 aluminum flat washers per coaster, each ⅝-inch (1.6 cm) diameter

1. Cut out as many vinyl coasters as you desire, each 4 x 4 inches (10.2 x 10.2 cm).

2. Following the contour of the molded design, use the scissors to round off the corners of the coasters.

3. Use the contact cement to adhere one washer to each raised circle on each vinyl coaster. Let the glue dry overnight.

Shimmering Circles

You Will Need
Aluminum flashing

Hot-glue gun and hot glue

Solid vinyl shelf liner

1. Measure and cut 10 strips of aluminum flashing for each coaster, each ¾ x 4 inches (1.9 x 10.2 cm).

2. Place five strips of cut flashing in a row with their long sides adjacent. Weave the remaining five strips over and under the first five strips.

3. Use the hot-glue gun to adhere the flashing strips together.

4. Cut the square piece of woven aluminum into a circle with a 4-inch (10.2 cm) diameter.

5. Draw a circle with a 4-inch (10.2 cm) diameter onto the shelf liner and cut out. Use the hot-glue gun to adhere the shelf liner circle onto the back side of the woven aluminum.

Retro Daisy

You Will Need

Carved wood rosette block, unfinished

Fine sandpaper

Acrylic craft paints in colors of your choice

Paintbrush

Clear, protective varnish

Self-adhesive felt (optional)

1. Remove all labels from the wood block. Lightly sand any areas where labels were removed.

2. Use the acrylic craft paint and brush to paint the background first; then paint the detailed areas you wish to highlight. Let the paint dry.

3. Seal the front and the back of the wood block with the clear varnish. If desired, cut a square of self-adhesive felt to fit the back of each coaster, and apply.

Vivacious Veneer

You Will Need

Wood veneer edging

4 shades of wood stain, such as oak, mahogany, maple, and walnut

Hot-glue gun and hot glue

Polyurethane spray, semi-gloss

Solid vinyl shelf liner

1. Measure and cut nine strips of the veneer edging for each coaster, each 3 ¾ inches (9.5 cm) long.

2. Following the manufacturer's instructions, stain the veneer strips. Stain three strips in one shade, and then stain two strips in each of the remaining three shades.

3. Alternate the stain colors as you line up five strips of the stained veneer edging. Weave the remaining four pieces of veneer perpendicularly through the five lined up. Use a hot-glue gun to adhere the strips together.

4. Spray three coats of the polyurethane onto the woven veneer. Let dry.

5. Cut a 3 ¾-inch (9.5 cm) square of the shelf liner. Use the hot-glue gun to adhere it to the back of the woven veneer.

What a Relief!

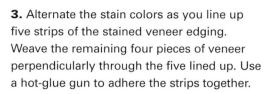

You Will Need

Aluminum flashing

Dry ballpoint pen

Ball-peen hammer

Sheet cork

Hot-glue gun and hot glue

1. Measure and cut out a 5 ½-inch (14 cm) square of aluminum flashing.

2. Measure ¾ inch (1.9 cm) in from each edge of the aluminum square. Use the dry ballpoint pen to draw a line all the way around the square at this point.

3. Cut off each corner of the square. On the dry pen line, fold the aluminum edge under to the back side.

4. Use the flat side of the hammer to flatten the folded lines. From the back side of the aluminum, use the ball-peen side of the hammer to pound a design into the center of the square.

5. Cut a piece of cork the same size as the hammered aluminum. Adhere it to the back side of the aluminum.

Bumper Bliss

You Will Need

1 ceramic tile, 4 x 4 inches (10.2 x 10.2 cm)

Multi-surface cleanser

Self-adhesive clear rubber picture frame bumpers, 36 per coaster

1. Remove all labels from the ceramic tile. Clean the surface of the tile with the cleanser.

2. Create the grid of clear rubber picture frame bumpers on the tile. One at a time, pull a bumper off its backing paper, position it on the tile, and then firmly press the bumper in place.

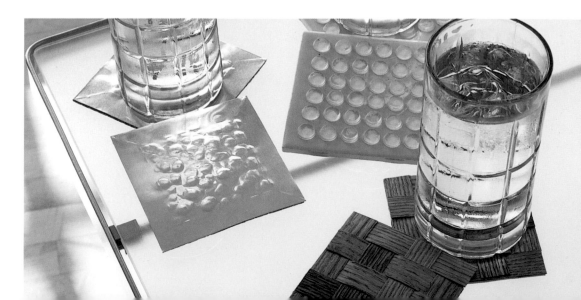

Lawn & Garden Department

A well-landscaped home is always more appealing. The funny thing is that you can use some of the same materials and tools that make the outside of your house look great on the inside, too. In this chapter, we'll show you clever new uses for such diverse items as lawn-mower parts, garden-hose hangers, pruning tools, potting containers, grill covers, and fencing accessories. If this list sounds intriguing to you, then explore the lawn and garden department, where creative home decorating ideas flourish as well as the many beautiful flowers, plants, and trees.

Tools

From full-size rakes and shovels to small weeders and trowels, there are plenty of handsome hand tools on the market. Many of these have metal heads attached to bleached wood, rubber, or plastic handles. On their own they are beautifully sculptural, yet with some creative installation, they can also serve a new purpose. Whether your decorating taste is strictly pastoral or uncompromisingly urban, these gardening tools can help cultivate your hardware style.

Pots & Containers

The fantastic selection of plant containers on the market is extraordinary in scope. Classic terra cotta, glazed ceramic, wood, metal, plastic, even hard foam—all these materials are getting their place in the sun. But there are more places they can rest, and more things they can hold, as you will soon discover.

Edgings, Arbors & Trellises

Edgings, arbors, and trellises are a great place to look for decor inspiration. Manufacturers are creating these products with much more attention to their aesthetic appeal. The level of design sophistication has risen so dramatically that you may be tempted to take home a length of edging, an arbor, or a trellis, and simply hang it on a wall, lay it on a table, or stick it in a pot as is.

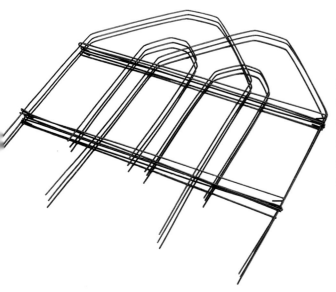

Outdoor Living Products

For many homeowners, decks, patios, and porches have become important living spaces, adding immeasurably to their quality of life. Whether you're hosting a casual cookout, watching the kids play in the yard, or simply enjoying private time lounging in the sun, time spent outside is precious indeed. Paying very close attention, home improvement centers jumped on this trend and now devote a complete section of their stores to providing an ample supply of outdoor-living products. From gas grills and portable fireplaces to tiki torches and holiday lights, these seasonal items really shine.

Cookbook Holder

Good cooks appreciate all the help they can get, and sometimes that help can come from the home improvement center. Originally intended to hold a garden hose, rope, or extension cord, this all-purpose garage hanger makes a divine cookbook holder. Simply open the book to the recipe you desire, and prop the top of the spine on the back metal bar. This way the book remains open to the page you desire, allowing you to focus on more important things, like not curdling your cream sauce!

The hanger has an epoxy finish that is rust resistant, so you can leave it out on countertops, wet or dry. For the utmost in luxury, stop bending to read recipes and install this hanger at eye level. All the mounting hardware is included with your purchase. If your cabinets are deep enough, you could even hang it on the back of the door. Just make sure the hanger is in close proximity to your working area.

To keep your cookbooks neat and clean, consider placing a piece of clear plexiglass in front of recipe while you are cooking. Squinting to decipher the fine print? Use a sheet of magnifying plastic; you can protect your pages and enlarge the book's type at the same time.

Both chic and inexpensive, this garden-variety gadget will soon be a favorite friend in the kitchen. Once you experience the convenience of a dependable cookbook holder, you'll wonder how you lived without one so long.

Baguette Bateau

Nothing complements a meal like a fresh, hot baguette, right out of the oven. Wrap it in a linen napkin to keep it warm and toss it in a—what? Just as you've invited everyone to take their places at the table, a painstakingly planned meal can get hurled into chaos when you don't have a reliable serving dish. Let this attractive container come to the rescue, straight from the lawn and garden department.

Purchase an oval planter, and you can use it directly off the shelf, lined with a pretty cloth napkin. The whitewashed raised rope and tassel pattern on this planter has the kind of classic elegance that would fit right in at an intimate candlelight dinner for two. Because it's made of a synthetic material, it is extremely light and won't scratch your furniture.

There are many other designs at the home improvement center from which to choose. A traditional unglazed terra-cotta version may be the answer for a casual cookout or family affair. Planters with interesting glaze colors or design patterns are available to suit any interior scheme you've created or any mood you wish to set. You also could personalize an inexpensive plastic vessel with paint. Let your imagination rise to any occasion!

Once dinner is over, just shake the crumbs out of the planter. This container is beautiful enough to store in the open, perhaps above a cabinet. You'll be glad to have it at arm's reach every time dinner's ready.

Unleashed Towel Bar

This eye-catching design features the cunning transformation of a dog's yard anchor into a kitchen-towel bar and pot-holder hook. Wood accents are painted apple red and attached to either end of the spiralling metallic anchor. Pipe straps not only secure the anchor to its base, but also allow it to pivot.

You Will Need

Drill with screwdriver bit

Drill bit, ⅜ inch (9.5 mm)

Wood ball, 2 ½-inch (6.4 cm) diameter

Gloss spray paint, red

Wood block, 5 x 3 x 1 inch (12.7 x 7.6 x 2.5 cm)

Heavy-duty glue

Dog anchor, 18 inches (45.7 cm)

3 galvanized pipe straps

Pliers

6 wood screws, ¾ inch (1.9 cm)

S hook

4 screws, 2 inches (5 cm)

1. Using the ⅜-inch (9.5 mm) bit, drill a hole in the wood ball that is ¾ inch (1.9 cm) deep.

2. Following the manufacturer's instructions, spray paint the wood ball and the wood block with the red paint. Multiple coats may be needed to achieve the color coverage you desire. Let the paint dry fully between coats.

3. Use the heavy-duty glue to adhere the drilled and painted ball onto the spiral end of the dog anchor. Let the glue dry.

4. Place a galvanized pipe strap over the triangle-shaped handle of the dog anchor. Use the pliers to pinch the strap ends together, leaving enough space for the anchor to pivot when screwed to the block. Repeat this process to attach the remaining two straps.

5. Attach the pipe straps to the wood block using the drill and the ¾-inch (1.9 cm) screws. Place the S hook in the leash circle to make the pot-holder hook. Use the four 2-inch (5 cm) screws to install the towel bar on the wall.

1. Select the highest-quality slotted cedar planter from the home improvement center. Look for one that is sturdy and built with the best wood. (Since these planters are very inexpensive, their features vary.)

2. Use the pliers to bend down or pull out any staples or wires protruding from the wood.

3. Thoroughly sand all the wood edges, curved corners, and flat surfaces to a smooth finish. (The cedar's rough veneer and many defects in the wood can be eliminated by careful sanding.) Wipe the sanded planter clean.

4. Following the manufacturer's instructions and working outdoors or in a well-ventilated area, spray paint the planter. Apply several thin coats of paint until you achieve the coverage you desire.

5. Cut the decorative image slightly smaller than the base of the planter. Mount the image on heavy card-stock paper if you wish. Slide the mounted image behind the planter's base wires.

Slotted Cedar Organizer

Make this great desktop filing system from a cedar planter by turning it on its side. Convenient gaps for envelopes, notepads, and pictures are built right into its slotted wood design. Smaller front holes store pencils, letter openers, and scissors. Well-placed metal wires hold a decorative image that covers the planter's base. Paint the wood any color you wish to complement your decor.

The rigid tines of a soil cultivator make excellent hooks on which to organize a myriad of objects. From kitchen utensils to key rings, anything with a large enough hole will slide on and off the tines with ease. Because they are built to aerate soil by penetrating hard ground, cultivators will withstand day-to-day use in even the busiest of homes.

This particular cultivator's two-tone duet of ash wood and chrome-plated steel is a handsome selection, yet there are many other handle varieties from which to choose, such as colorful plastic, painted metal, or grooved rubber. Just pick whatever appeals to you.

Installing three cultivators in a row does require a little more wall space, but this arrangement conveniently triples your storage capacity while looking exceptionally artful. Good-bye overcrowded drawers; hello modern masterpiece.

Helpful Hang-Ups

Everyone is allowed one junk drawer; that's a given. But when you get poked by a shish-kebab skewer while looking for a slotted spoon, it's time to clear away the clutter. Here is one simple idea that might be the key to some overdue organization.

Wheelie Paper Towel Holder

Scale, color, and texture are essential to good design. The unusual size of these little lawn mower tires coupled with their shiny rubber treads and white enamel wheels are irresistable and inspiring. By attaching one tire onto each end of a metal pipe, you can create this unique paper towel holder. It can sit vertically or horizontally on a counter, or even be hung by a chain. Let this racy accessory jump-start your decorating ideas for the kitchen, workshop, or garage.

You Will Need

Hacksaw *

Threaded metal rod, ⅝-inch (1.6 cm) diameter

Metal file

4 hex nuts to fit threaded rod

2 small lawn mower tires

Paper towels

* see 10 Things You Should Know about Using a Hacksaw, page 132

1. Use the hacksaw to cut a 15-inch (38.1 cm) piece of the threaded metal rod. Lightly file the cut end of the rod.

2. Screw a hex nut onto one end of the rod and twist it 2 to 3 inches (5 to 7.6 cm) up the threads (enough room for one tire to fit on the rod). Feed the tire onto the rod. Screw a second nut onto the rod to secure the tire in place at the end of the rod. Adjust the upper nut as needed to make a tight connection.

3. Place the paper towel roll on the rod. Screw a hex nut onto the opposite end of the rod and slightly down its length. Put the second tire on the rod, and then secure it in place with the final hex nut. Adjust the nuts as needed to make a tight connection.

10 things you should know about using a hacksaw

1. Wear safety glasses or goggles and work gloves.

2. Use the correct blade for the type of metal being cut.

3. Securely install the blade with its teeth pointing forward.

4. Make sure the blade remains rigid and the saw frame is properly aligned.

5. Saw away from yourself with strong, steady strokes.

6. Saw harder metals more slowly than softer metals.

7. Use a light machine oil on the blade to prevent it from overheating and breaking.

8. Use a clamp when sawing the edges of thin, flat metal.

9. Store saws with clean and protected blades.

10. Clean up all metal shards from your work area.

Charcoal Laundry Bag

As a playful example of redirected use, here's an outdoor grill cover turned upside down and converted into an extra-large laundry bag. Its decorative motif is inspired by washing instruction icons and executed with strips of silver and white duct tape.

You Will Need

Grill cover with elastic closure

Iron, ironing board, and towel (optional)

Utility knife

Metal ruler

Wooden cutting board or other firm cutting surface

Silver duct tape, 2 inches (5 cm) wide

Circle template, 2 inches (5 cm) or less in diameter

White duct tape, 2 inches (5 cm) wide

Large heavy books

1. If the plastic grill cover is wrinkled, stretch it over an ironing board, place a damp towel on top, and use a hot iron to steam out the wrinkles.

2. Use the utility knife and metal ruler on top of the cutting board to cut enough strips of the silver duct tape to replicate the pattern shown on page 141.

3. Adhere the strips of silver duct tape to the front of the plastic grill cover in the shapes shown.

4. Position the circle template on a strip of the white duct tape on the cutting board. Use the utility knife to cut the tape around the template. Adhere the white duct tape circles to the grill cover.

5. Lay the bag on a flat surface, such as an ironing board, and smooth out the decorated area. Position large heavy books over the surface, and leave them in place overnight to secure the bond.

Cagey Lamp

Garden center supplies support this ultra-mod floor lamp. Two cone-shaped tomato cages are covered with poultry wire; then their larger holes are connected, giving the lamp an organic shape. Blanketing the wire with multiple layers of thin paper dipped in glue is jolly good fun. You'll enjoy making this one-of-a-kind floor lamp as much as you will living with it for years to come.

You Will Need

Wire cutters

2 wire tomato cages

Work gloves

Poultry wire

Galvanized wire, 24 gauge

Pliers

Electrical light kit or clamp work light

Kozo, rice, or tissue papers

White craft glue

Plastic sheeting

Latex gloves

Acrylic medium (optional)

Rubber stoppers

1. Use wire cutters to remove the legs from one of the tomato cages.

2. Wearing the work gloves, unroll a length of poultry wire. Wrap it around the outside of the tomato cage to determine how long a piece you need, and then cut off that length of poultry wire.

3. Shape the poultry wire around the tomato cage with pliers. Secure it to the top and bottom of the tomato cage with short lengths of galvanized wire. Trim excess poultry wire from the top and bottom of the tomato cage, and set it aside.

4. Follow steps 2 and 3 to wrap and secure a second length of poultry wire around the second tomato cage.

5. Wire the electrical light fixture on the inside of the tomato cage with legs. (We used a clamp work light suspended inside the cage by wire.)

6. Wire the two wire-wrapped cages together.

7. Tear the kozo, rice, or tissue paper into 2-inch-wide (5 cm) strips. Set them aside.

8. Mix a solution of one part white craft glue to two parts water.

9. Spread the plastic sheeting on the floor (this is the messy part!). Wearing the latex gloves, dip a strip of paper in the glue mixture, and then lay the strip on the poultry wire surface. Add many more strips to cover the cages, overlapping the paper as you go. Let the strips dry on the lamp overnight.

10. Cover the lamp with a second layer of glued paper strips. Let it dry. (We created stripes on our lamp with a second color of paper, added last.)

11. If desired, coat the outside of the lamp with an acrylic medium. Stick one black rubber stopper on the bottom of each wire leg.

Reflector Magnets

These funky refrigerator magnets jazz up any setting with sparkling bursts of pure color. Made from outdoor reflectors, they're extremely visible, durable, and waterproof. When a light is shined upon them, outdoor reflectors draw attention to objects in the dark. They're often installed on fences, posts, and mailboxes to alert the attention of oncoming traffic. Assemble your own set of reflector magnets in a flash, and put their dazzling energy to use indoors.

You Will Need

Mini-reflectors in assorted colors, each 1 ¼-inch (3.2 cm) diameter, (self-adhesive if available)

Round magnets, 1-inch (2.5 cm) diameter, ¼ inch (6 mm) thick*

Multi-purpose epoxy (optional)

*Home improvement centers and craft supply stores sell magnets in several forms. Some types are self-adhesive; they're manufactured on a backing paper that, once removed, exposes a sticky surface. Some magnets you'll have to glue yourself. Magnets sold in sheet and strip form can be cut to any size or shape, while other magnets, particularly the thicker and stronger ones, are sold in precut forms.

If you're using self-adhesive mini-reflectors or magnets, simply center one magnet on the back side of each reflector and firmly press it in place. If your reflectors or magnets are not self-adhesive, use a multi-purpose epoxy to bond the two elements.

window treats

Often small parts of your home's decor can make big impressions. Window treatments—not the fabric, but the hardware—are the type of detail that typically could use more attention. With just a little creative thinking, you can design one-of-a-kind accessories to dress up your windows. Instead of settling for mass-produced solutions for hanging up and holding back curtains and sheers, why not investigate innovative options from the home improvement center aisles? You'll be glad you did. Here are just a few possibilities to spark your imagination.

Get Hooked

Heavy-duty storage hooks come in many shapes and sizes. They're used for hanging weighty items, such as bicycles, ladders, and yard tools, mainly in garage, basement, and attic areas. Some utility hooks are coated in brightly colored plastic that delivers a zesty visual twist. The bicycle storage hook shown (above, left) screws directly into the wall; once installed, all you have to do is drape your curtain behind its curve.

Leg Look

You can find a variety of milled chair legs near the lumber department of your home improvement center. These unfinished accessories can be straight or spindled, short and squat or tall and slender. To use one as a curtain holder, simply paint or stain the wood to suit your style, and then screw its bolt into an anchor in your wall.

Simply Chain

In general, there are two kinds of chain: one that carries heavy loads, and one that's purely decorative. However, we think these categories aren't mutually exclusive. Although the straight-link welded chain pictured is surely sturdy and can perform many tasks, it's also extremely attractive. Its subtle gleam and simple links make it particularly sophisticated, especially when looped around and tying back a curtain.

Doorstop Drama

Here's a smart new look for tab-top curtains. Instead of feeding every tab onto a single rod, you can loop individual tabs over a series of doorstops. Installing the stops at regular intervals above a window frame ensures the curtain will always hang in neat, orderly folds. Mark your wall to indicate the position of each doorstop, and then just screw them in. This speedy makeover won't hamper your schedule or break your budget, and you'll love the theatrical results.

A Pipe Supreme

Install this impressive curtain rod, and you can achieve the exposed-pipe look so frequently seen (and lusted after) in renovated warehouses. To get the job done you'll need a metal pipe, two 90-degree elbow joints, and two flanges. These plumbing supplies can be any diameter you choose; just make sure they're galvanized for rust-resistance and sheen. Join the connectors, slip the curtains on the pipe, and mount the flanges into ceiling joists for maximum support.

Templates

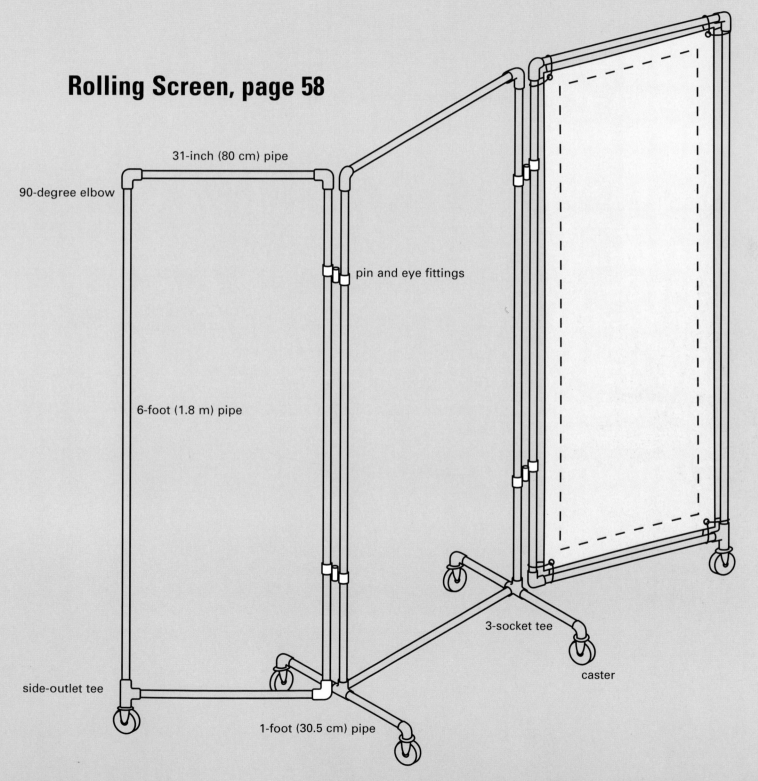

Rolling Screen, page 58

31-inch (80 cm) pipe

90-degree elbow

pin and eye fittings

6-foot (1.8 m) pipe

3-socket tee

caster

side-outlet tee

1-foot (30.5 cm) pipe

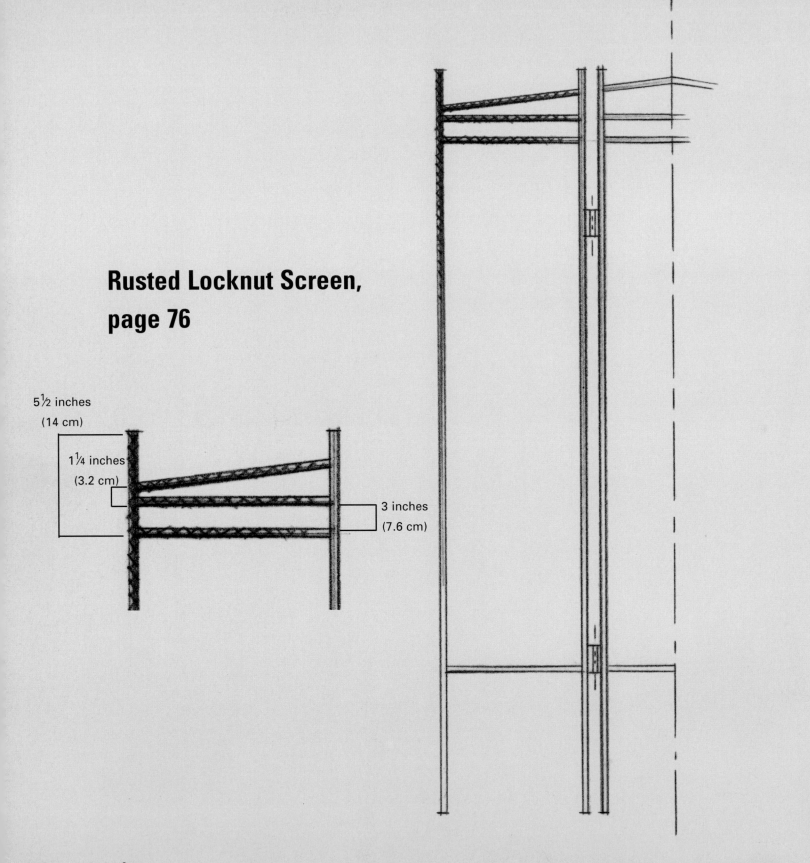

**Rusted Locknut Screen,
page 76**

5½ inches
(14 cm)

1¼ inches
(3.2 cm)

3 inches
(7.6 cm)

Charcoal Laundry Bag, page 132

Enlarge 500%

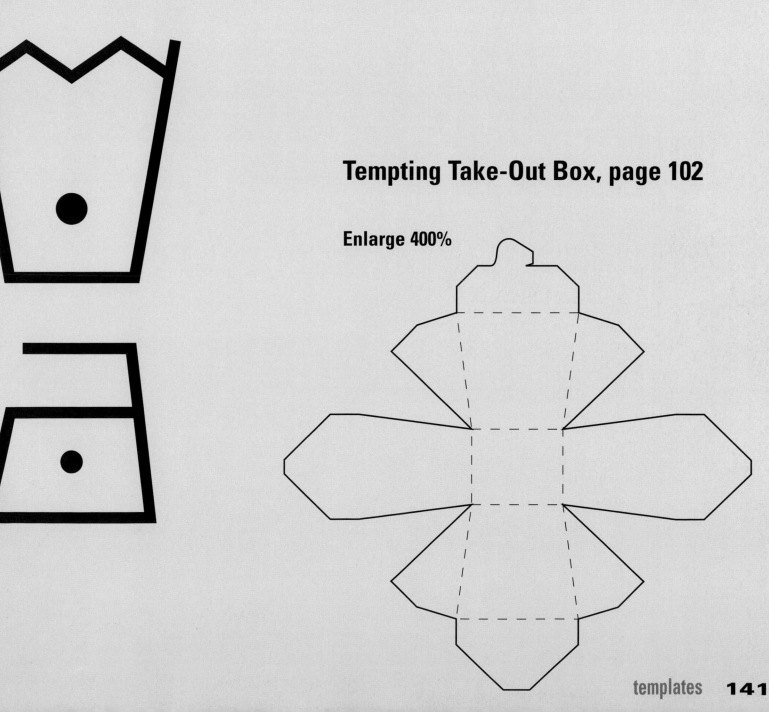

Tempting Take-Out Box, page 102

Enlarge 400%

Contributing Designers

Trulee Grace Hall is a multimedia artist and musician who makes her home in Asheville, North Carolina. Spanning the genres of visual, performing, and musical arts, Trulee's work includes calendar and greeting card production; furniture, clothing, and set design; interior decoration and restoration; painting and sculpture; video production; large-scale installation; and audio production and recording. Trulee also finds time to run a community art space in downtown Asheville, spotlighting the area's less conventional local talent. Most importantly, Trulee loves and cares for her aging dog friend, Loolee.

Joan Morris' artistic endeavors have led her down many successful creative paths. A childhood interest in sewing turned into professional costuming for motion pictures. After studying ceramics, Joan ran her own clay wind chime business for 15 years. Since 1993, Joan's Asheville, North Carolina coffee house, Vincent's Ear, has provided a vital meeting place for all varieties of artists and thinkers. As a frequent designer for Lark Books, Joan's projects recently have been featured in *Beautiful Ribbon Crafts* (Spring 2003), *The Weekend Crafter: Dried Flower Crafts* (Spring 2003), *Gifts for Babies* (Spring 2003), *Halloween: A Grown-up's Guide to Creative Costumes, Devilish Decor & Fabulous Festivities* (Fall 2003), and *Creating Fantastic Vases* (Fall 2003).

Heather Smith is a teacher, freelance writer, and project designer in Asheville, North Carolina. She enjoys assignments that allow her to enhance and beautify overlooked and ordinary objects, people, and places—especially, when the process requires her to make a mess and get dirty.

Terry Taylor is the principal in-house craft designer for Lark Books. Projects from Terry's abundant and resourseful imagination are featured in many Lark publications, in addition to the ones he writes and edits. In his life outside of Lark, Terry is well-respected as a multimedia artist and jeweler.

Acknowledgments

Many people devoted their time and talents to make this book. I offer my heartfelt thanks for their creativity, labor, and encouragement.

Tom Metcalf's keen sense of style is visible on every page. Thanks for your passionate art direction. Keith Wright and Wendy Wright enthusiastically and efficiently captured glorious images. Thanks to you both.

Betty Lou Jeffrey, Judith and Jim Burt, Judy and Mike Mayer, Kathryn Philpott Hill, and Richard Fort graciously welcomed us into their remarkable homes. We deeply appreciate the opportunity to work in such beautiful locations. Thanks also to Bobby Gold for coordinating our location access. You can visit his website at www.orbitmodern.com.

Delores Gosnell kept all the administrative details in order. Many thanks for your flawless organization and friendly smiles. Sherry Hames has come through for me again with her exceptional word skills. I appreciate the great care with which she refines my writing.

Chris Bryant, Trulee Grace Hall, Heather Smith, and Terry Taylor each brought their stylish designs to life with skilled workmanship and flair. Thanks for your incredible projects.

This book is dedicated to Joan Morris, my principal designer and dear friend. From day one, her commitment to this project has been an inspiration. Together, as we prowled the home center aisles for what seemed an eternity, the intensity of her creative spirit and good humor never faltered. These marvelous traits are the essence of her character and just a small part of what makes her such a special friend.

Notes About Suppliers

Usually, the supplies you need for making the projects in Lark books can be found at your local craft supply store, discount mart, home improvement center, or retail shop that relevant to the topic of the book. Occasionally, however, you may need to buy materials or tools from specialty suppliers. In order to provide you with the most up-to-date information, we have created a listing of suppliers on our website, which we update on a regular basis. Visit us at www.larkbooks.com; click on "Craft Supply Sources;" and then click on the relevant topic. You will find numerous companies listed with their website address and/or mailing address and phone number.

Index

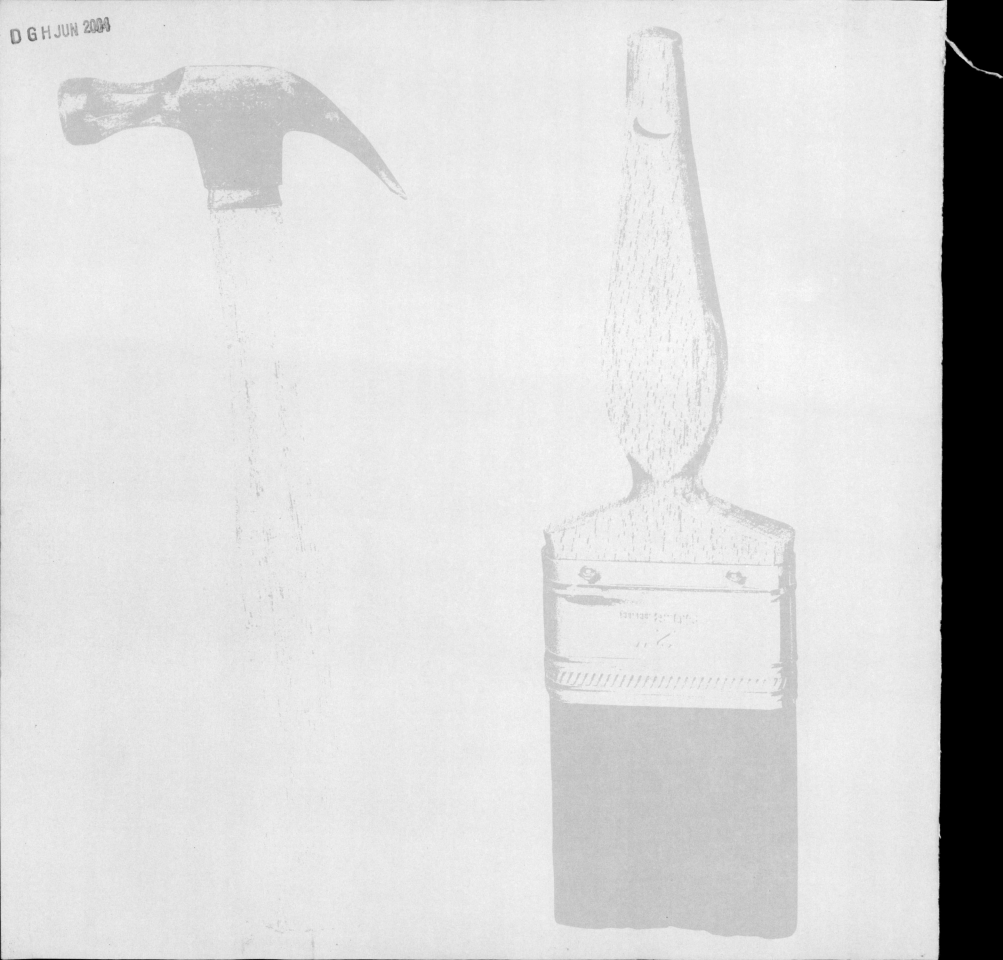